# Starting a
# Nursery or Herb Farm

# Starting a
# Nursery or Herb Farm

**John Mason**

© John Mason 1983 and 1997

Photography by John Mason and David Miller
Editorial Assistant: Iain Harrison

National Library of Australia
Cataloguing-in-Publication Data

Mason, John, 1951-
Starting a Nursery or Herb Farm
Rev.ed.
Bibliography.
Includes index.
ISBN 0 86417 843 3

1. Nurseries (Horticulture) — Management.
I. Title.
635'.068

First published 1983 by Night Owl Press
Second Edition published 1997 by Kangaroo Press Pty Ltd
3 Whitehall Road Kenthurst NSW 2156 Australia
PO Box 6125 Dural Delivery Centre NSW 2158 Australia
Printed by The Australian Print Group, Maryborough VIC 3465

# Contents

# Introduction

This book is written as a guide or handbook for the person attempting to start or run a nursery or herb farm. It does not give all the information you might need or want, but it does cover all the important aspects of the topic. Use this book as a guide, a starting point, maybe a reference to come back to, but look at other information as well. Study closely the herb farm or nursery industry in your part of the country. Speak with appropriate government departments such as agriculture, forestry and CSIRO. Speak with horticultural clubs, colleges and schools. All of these places can help you with the detailed information you need to acquire about your chosen sector of the industry.

It is very important for you to realise that there are tremendous variations in the way plants are treated from place to place. Information in this book is relevant to 'average' Australia or New Zealand, if there is such a place. In general, information is relevant to climates similar to Sydney, Adelaide, Perth, Canberra or Melbourne. In warmer or cooler climates, you may need to modify the recommendations to some extent.

Always remember that every plant is an individual. Ten different plants grown from the same batch of seed are different. They differ in their shape and growth rate, their disease-resistance and their nutrient and water requirements. Bear in mind also that the same plant requires different treatment in different places and at different times of the year. Whenever reading any book on gardening (propagation or any other discipline), consider where the author's experience has been gained. Information written by a Melbourne gardener, unless stated otherwise, is probably only fully relevant to Melbourne.

Any person running a herb farm or nursery is going to need to use several books for reference and it is important to know that reference books are accurate. Once again consider the author's background and training. The books most likely to provide credible information must always be those written by people with both solid academic training plus extensive practical experience in the subject. There are many valuable publications written by people who have only the practical experience. Beware of books written by artists, journalists and engineers, who sometimes write gardening books simply because they're interested in the subject and happen to have the 'contacts' through writing on other subjects. A gardening book by an artist or architect can be a beautiful coffee-table publication, but in terms of accuracy for reference, can lead to disaster.

## PLANT CLASSIFICATION

Despite the fact that every plant is an individual, some plants do share characteristics to a greater or smaller degree, and they are classified on the basis of such similarities.

Plants are known by both common and scientific names. Unfortunately, the same plant can often have many different common names or many different plants can have the same common name. This situation has, in the main, made the use of common names confusing and often unreliable. The confusion is not so marked with herbs, however — perhaps because of their long history of use — and herbs are often sold only under the common name, whereas most other plants are usually grown and sold under their scientific name.

Scientific names, being in Latin, may initially be more difficult to learn, but they are totally reliable. Any one plant has only one scientific name. In this system, plants are classified by dividing them into groups with even closer similarities and so on. There are seven levels of division:

All plants are divided into several *phyla*
Phyla are divided into *classes*
Classes are divided into *orders*
Orders are divided into *families*
Families are divided into *genera* (singular: *genus*)
Genera are divided into *species*
Species are divided into *varieties*.

When identifying a plant we use the genus and species names (and if applicable the variety) e.g. *Eucalyptus* (genus) *camaldulensis* (species).

Correct identification and labelling of plants is essential. Help with the identification of plants can be obtained from botanic gardens, university botany departments or your government herbarium (in most capital cities).

# The Alternatives

There are a number of very basic decisions which need to be made before commencing a herb farm or nursery operation. These alternatives should be reconsidered every year or two through an operation, and perhaps changes made accordingly. These first decisions are discussed in turn below.

## FORM OF PRODUCT

Most nurseries and herb farms specialise in one or two of the following products.

### Plants in Pots

This is the way the major part of the herb farm and nursery industries operate. The scale at which this sector of the industry operates makes growing in containers a low-risk operation compared with some other alternatives. Plants in containers do, however, become potbound and need to be sold or else potted up within a certain time.

### Plants in the Open Ground

Plants are grown in cultivated paddocks until ready for sale, at which time they are dug up and prepared for sale in various ways:

— they are put into containers

— soil is removed from the roots (deciduous plants only) and they are stored over winter with roots in moistened shavings or straw

— the soil ball is held together by tying hessian around it

— in some heavier soils, plants are sold with whatever soil clings to the roots left as such, not contained in any way by cloth or any other container.

After container growing this is the next most common practice. Open-ground growing is economical in that it doesn't require the same expense for containers and usually it calls for less watering.

### Bare Rooted Cuttings

Some nurseries specialise in propagation, that is producing roots on cuttings. They leave the job of growing the plants up to a saleable size to another

Herbal products such as cosmetics, herb vinegars, pomanders, and dried herbs for cooking are becoming ever more popular, but do not rely on them heavily at first — business may take time to build up.

nursery. This type of operation requires less area but more expertise and a greater initial outlay on expensive propagating structures and equipment.

## Specialised Container Products

Hanging baskets, terrariums, bonsai, mini-gardens and plants in decorative tubs are all products in which a nursery can specialise. Before commencing this type of operation however, study carefully the demands of the market and know what competition exists.

You also need to be sure you know how to produce your product and how to produce it well. Anyone can make a bonsai, but it takes skill to make a good one which will survive.

## Herbal Products

There is a definite growth in demand for such things as dried herbs, teas, oils, candles and pillows. Compared to the broad nursery industry, however, this industry is minute. You should be careful about depending too heavily on this type of operation. It is more sensible to start as a sideline and grow, than to throw everything you have into producing a line of herbal products.

Plants grown in the open ground may be sold in several ways including, as shown here, with a soil ball attached to the roots.

# GROWTH STAGE

At what stages of the plant's development will you be handling the plant? The answer could be either one or a combination of the following stages.

## Propagation

The beginning of the plant's life: seed is sown, a cutting is struck, bulbs are divided or a fruit tree is budded, etc. This stage requires greater technical skill and, in some cases, more expensive equipment than other stages.

## Planting Out

The small propagated plants are put into pots, planted into the open ground or into some other situation in which they can be grown to a larger size. There is more difficulty at the beginning of this operation when the plants are moved from a pampered propagating environment to a harsher growing-on environment. As they become older, they harden and become more resistant to disease and environmental problems.

## Advanced Growing

This involves growing plants to a large size either in containers or the open ground. Though these plants might be hardy, this type of work is heavy and usually requires at least some machinery to handle the plants.

Many nurseries supplement their sales of plants with ancillary products — pots, window boxes, watering cans, and various sprays and treatments.

## QUANTITY

On what scale will you operate? Will it be a one person part-time or full-time business or will several people be engaged full-time? The quantity of plants handled annually will depend very much on the stages of the nursery or herb farm operation (outlined above) in which you are involved. A propagation nursery needs to produce up to 100,000 cuttings a year to be a reasonable operation for one person. A nursery which does everything from propagation through to retailing can be a feasible operation for one individual producing as few as 10,000 plants a year.

## QUALITY

This raises such questions as the type of label (with a photograph, printed or simply handwritten), type of container (cheap plastic bag, simple solid plastic pot or better-looking plastic pot), whether plants are sold with a stake or trellis, and whether plants will be pruned to shape as part of the growing process. Will plants which don't thrive be thrown out or still sold? Will potbound plants be sold? It is not necessary to decide all these details at the planning stage, but you should formulate a general policy on quality.

## SELLING

The first decision to make is whether your operation is to be wholesale (selling to retailers or resellers) or retail (selling direct to the general public). Retail operations are generally more demanding in terms of time, but give a better return per plant. A retail nursery or herb farm must be attended at the advertised opening times irrespective of whether customers are there or not. It is difficult for someone running a one-person retail operation ever to have time to take a holiday, whereas a person running a wholesale operation needs only to employ a person on a part-time basis to so some watering for times such as annual leave.

You should aim at growing your produce for a particular market. Consider the following alternatives:

—your local area, your region or perhaps interstate. Interstate sales (southern states) are appropriate for 'indoor' or tropical plants grown in Queensland.

—bulk users of plants such as council parks departments, housing estates, landscapers, farmers etc.

—supermarket chains and other large business organisations

—home gardeners. Even here you may decide to aim at inner suburban, outer suburban or country markets.

Plants can be sold both retail and wholesale by a number of alternative methods.

The greater part of the nursery industry operates by selling plants in pots. Seedlings, especially vegetables, may be grown in trays and sold for planting out simply wrapped in cloth or newspaper.

## Mail Order Sales
Sales are conducted either by advertising in magazines or by sending lists or catalogues to prospective customers through the mail, but it is very important that they are packaged in a proper way to avoid damage.

## Roadside and Market Sales
These involve setting up a temporary stand which you operate only when you have something to sell. This type of operation is usually small-scale, but can be a very worthwhile supplement or contribution as a part income. It is rarely, by itself, a satisfactory way to earn a complete income.

## Permanent Outlet
This is the most common, most demanding and most profitable way of conducting any type of sale.

## Truck Sales
One of the most common wholesale selling methods is to make regular visits to a round of retail establishments in a truck carrying a selection of plants or other products. The retailers view the merchandise and buy direct off the truck. This system can be difficult for the beginner, but once you learn what plants or herb products are most likely to sell, then you can be almost assured of complete sales before starting your round.

Market sales can yield a useful supplementary income, but are rarely sufficient to provide a living.

## Contract Sales

Some government departments, supermarket chains and other large organisations will enter into contracts with nurseries to propagate and grow specified numbers of certain varieties of plants. Some retail or 'growing-on' nurseries will sign contracts with propagation nurseries to supply them with plants at some future date. This way of selling is more certain for the nurseryman, but usually pays less per plant.

## Export Sales

Some Australian nurseries do a significant amount of business by selling plants to other countries. Because of transport, and quarantine restrictions, this business tends to be restricted to certain types of plants. Overseas markets are very large compared with Australia; and there are always collectors who are prepared to pay well for products they can't easily obtain in their own country.

# Management
# and Organisation

To work efficiently and profitably, a nursery or herb farm must be both well organised and properly managed in a clear conscious manner. As with most other businesses, it is essential to be confident enough to make firm decisions when they are needed. The nursery or herb farmer who takes too long to make decisions is almost certain to fail.

## SELECTING THE SITE

It is not always possible to have the ideal site. Sometimes a piece of land is already owned or perhaps financial limitations force a compromise. Important considerations are discussed on the following page.

If your site is not ideal, you can at least make the most of it: terracing using railway sleepers creates beds in the sloping ground around this shadehouse.

## To Own or Rent

If money is to be borrowed for any part of the operation, land is a better proposition for a loan than most other things. Consider the permanency of your operation. Land ownership is considered a less flexible means of operation than renting. Renting, however, can be an insecure form of tenure.

## Size of Site

Generally, nurseries or herb farms require significantly less land than other types of primary production. Propagation nurseries and retail operations can be successfully conducted on less than half a hectare. Standard container growing of herbs or other plants is usually conducted on about a hectare. Some of the largest container nurseries in Australia can run on less than two to three hectares because they are carefully organised and managed. Open-ground nurseries can be anything from a few to more than a hundred hectares.

## Proximity to Market

A retail business is best located on a major road travelled frequently by large numbers of prospective customers or, alternatively, in a centre which is frequented by prospective customers. Avoid locating too close to similar existing businesses. If wholesaling, locate within reasonable proximity to customers, or to existing transportation networks (e.g. a mail-order nursery selling throughout Australia could successfully establish close to any reasonable railway station).

## Availability of Water

All plants need water to grow, but some need more than others. A reliable source of unpolluted, water low in salts is essential.

## Fertile Soil

This is only really important when growing in the open ground. Good container nurseries can be established in very infertile areas.

## Climate

If establishing in an unsatisfactory climate for the plants being grown, extra expense will need to be incurred on developing climatic controls (glasshouses, windbreaks and shadehouses).

## Availability of Materials

In container nurseries, in particular, it is important to be close to a reliable source of material which can be used in potting mixes. Cartage costs on sand, loam, pine bark and other such materials can be significant, so always check what is involved before ordering anything.

A successful nursery business does not necessarily require large premises: this setup operates from a house block in the middle of a city.

A well-travelled road is an ideal location; this country nursery attracts many retail customers with a well-placed sign.

Many shops supplement their sales with a nursery department, and an outside display can secure many casual sales to passers-by.

20

# SELECTING THE CROP

All too often, people enter horticulture with very definite prejudged ideas on what they will grow, where they will grow it and how they will grow it. While such people have a real advantage in that they obviously love that particular type of plant, they can only benefit by giving objective consideration to *all* the alternatives.

Crops grown by nurseries fall into the following broad categories:

INDOOR OR TROPICAL PLANTS: grown outside in the northern parts of Australia; the same are often grown indoors in cooler parts.

NATIVES: plants indigenous to Australia.

PERENNIALS: soft-wooded (herbaceous) plants grown for decoration.

BULBS: also corms, rhizomes and tubers grown for flower, often with perennials.

EXOTIC ORNAMENTALS: woody plants not native to Australia, grown for nonproductive or amenity purposes. Often nurseries specialise in one particular group of exotics (e.g. azaleas, geraniums or cacti).

FRUIT AND NUTS: deciduous fruit tree nurseries usually also grow deciduous ornamental trees which require similar techniques and treatment. Some specialise in citrus or berries.

The principal choice facing the herb farmer involves the form in which the crops will be sold:

PLANTS FOR SALE: either grown in containers or in the ground.

CROPPING: herbs grown *en masse,* the foliage being cropped and perhaps dried or oil extracted for sale.

HERB PRODUCTS: growing plants to provide the raw material to produce a range of herbal products (e.g. teas, dried herbs, candles and preserves).

When considering the alternative crops there are a number of questions to which you must find the answers.

How well does the product keep? If it can't be sold immediately, can it be potted up? Will it still be saleable in a month or a year?

How long does it take to become saleable? Some operations (e.g. selling 5 cm tube-size plants) can give a return in three or four months from starting, while others (e.g. citrus trees) can take up to seven years from starting the rootstock to selling the potted plant.

What will be your peak work times? Different types of operations will impose heavy or light workloads at different times of the year. Deciduous plants require budding in February–March and digging for sale in winter. The remainder of the year is lighter work. Retail nurseries or herb farms are very busy in spring and to a lesser degree in autumn, although summer is very slow.

Working in groups is congenial, but is not necessarily the most efficient way of completing a task. Sensible management of labour time can mean the difference between success and failure.

Starting small is always a wise policy — this home-made shadehouse of brush has been built to allow for expansion. The tree in the corner gives useful extra shade.

What are you most capable of doing? Don't attempt to grow difficult plants if you are relatively inexperienced. Don't grow indoor plants in Melbourne unless you have the glasshouses to do so.

What demand exists for the product? Is that demand constant or is it likely to increase or perhaps decrease?

Will you specialise or combine a number of different alternatives?

There is a tendency toward specialisation but perhaps for the beginner, a more general approach is of less risk.

What will be the costs and initial outlay, and how do they compare with the return? Some types of operation (e.g. indoor plants in cooler climates) require very large initial outlays.

## LAYOUT

In any nursery or herb farm, the plants or herb products leaving the site is the culmination of many different stages. An efficient operation necessitates a smooth and easy flow from one step to the next. It is necessary to identify the

Running a nursery involves many hours of repetitive tasks, and the importance of a pleasant and spacious working environment should never be underestimated.

various components (e.g. seed or cutting material, pots and potting mix) which are coming together to produce the final product. These components must be arranged so that they come together with the minimum of effort.

When planning the layout of your operation, you should decide on the areas needed for different tasks. The nursery plan should include adequate space for the following;

— stock plants (plants from which cuttings and perhaps seed are collected)
— store for pots, fertiliser, barrows and the like
— soil bins for material to be used in potting media
— propagation area where seed and cuttings are planted into pots
— glasshouse for getting seed and cuttings started
— area for mixing potting media
— potting-up area
— growing-on area, where plants are grown to full size after seed or cuttings are put in individual pots
— despatch area, where orders for wholesaling are collected and loaded onto a truck for despatch.

It is important to have different work and storage areas integrated into a flow pattern, so consider the relationship between these areas and decide their relative proximity. For example:

— the propagation and potting-up areas could possibly be in the same place
— the store needs to be near a road so that delivery vans can easily unload
— the soil bins also need easy access to roads
— the soil bins should be located adjacent to the area for mixing pottings soils
— the area for potting up should be adjacent to the area for growing on which in turn should be adjacent to the area for despatch.

Decisions on these details once made should be written down. Take a plan of the site as it exists showing fixed features such as building, waterpipes, electricity wires, fences and trees, and try to arrange the various areas to achieve most of the desired relationships you have decided upon.

Once the approximate location of each area has been decided, the fine detail of the way each area is to be organised can be worked out.


## MANAGING MANPOWER, EQUIPMENT AND MATERIALS

No matter how tedious it might seem, it is essential that you write things down on paper. When starting a new operation, planning is required for manpower, equipment and materials both in terms of the amount required (otherwise you have too much or too little) and how they are best used.

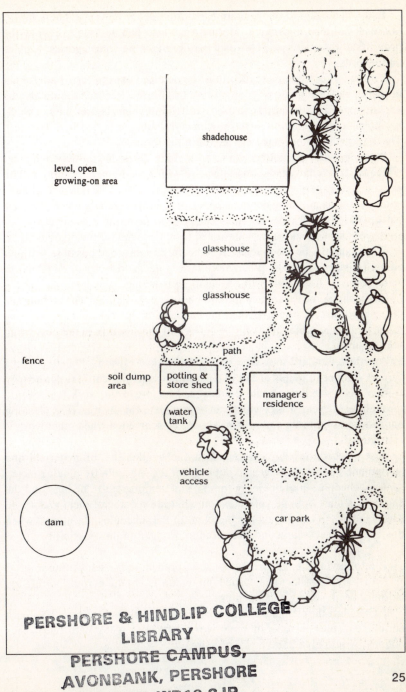

level, open
growing-on area

shadehouse

glasshouse

glasshouse

path

fence

soil dump
area

potting &
store shed

manager's
residence

water
tank

vehicle
access

dam

car park

Later, in the day-to-day operation, records need to be kept not only for the tax man, but also to provide information which can be used to review the progress of the operation. This paperwork falls into two categories — plans and records.

You must keep complete records of income and expenditure (both for tax purposes and as a guide to your success or failure). Records should also be kept of materials purchased and used, staff, (if someone is fired make a note), accidents and production rates (how many plants are potted in a day etc.). These records can become very useful in the future.

Plans include scheduling work and making decisions on the equipment which will be required and on the way in which the nursery or farm will be expanded. It is very easy to find yourself making plans like this in your head without putting anything down on paper. It is, however, only when plans are worked through on paper that they can be seen in a proper perspective.

A work schedule should be designed to achieve the following objectives:

Work should be completed for the minimum cost possible without compromising standards. When more money needs to be spent on labour to achieve only a little more work, something is wrong.

Work should be completed in minimum time. In nurseries or herb farms, the worker can easily be distracted and become involved in unnecessary fussy tasks — such as smoothing out the surface of the soil mix in the pots while potting up.

A certain standard should be stated and worked towards. Plan to pot up a certain number of plants or put in a certain numbers of cuttings per hour.

The work schedule should be designed to spread the work load evenly throughout the year. Tasks which can be completed at any time (e.g. cleaning out a store or building a new dam) should be scheduled when other work is at minimum.

When scheduling, give thought to the availability of materials and equipment, so that shortages do not prevent the schedule from being met.

The schedule should be easy to read and comprehend. The boss and the employees must both be very clear on what is expected of them and when. There should, of course, always be room for the schedule to be altered when this becomes necessary, and staff need to be clear on this possibility.

The following steps represent a useful procedure for scheduling.

1. List all the tasks to be carried out over a 12-month period (potting up, cuttings, seed, selling and weeding).

2. Calculate the estimated number of man-hours available over a 12-month period (e.g. one person full time over 50 hours a week with two weeks holiday, would give 2500 hours of work).

3. Allocate the hours available to the jobs needed to be done.

4. Make up a table on a large sheet of paper listing the tasks or jobs in the column on the left-hand side and the weeks of the year across the top.

5. Allocate the hours available to each task throughout the weeks of the year in a way which will spread the work as evenly as possible throughout the year.

---

### Example - Section of a Work Schedule (Times in Hours)

| Week | 1. | 2. | 3. | 4. | 5. | 6. | 7. | 8. | 9. |
|---|---|---|---|---|---|---|---|---|---|
| Seed | | 10 | 10 | | | 4 | | | |
| Pricking | | 10 | 8 | 10 | 12 | 8 | | | |
| Potting | 12 | 15 | 8 | 20 | 20 | 16 | 3 | | |
| Moving Plants | 4 | | | | | | | | 1 |
| Washing Pots | 4 | | | | 4 | | | | |
| Mixing Soil | 12 | | | 10 | | | | | |
| Order Materials | 4 | | | | | | 1 | | |
| Selling | | | 8 | | | 8 | 16 | 8 | 8 |
| Bookwork | 4 | 1 | | | | 4 | | | 1 |

# Propagating Techniques:
# An Overview

Broadly, there are two ways of propagating plants — asexually and sexually.

Asexual propagation involves growing a new plant from some part (e.g. leaf, stem and root) of an existing plant. This is also known as *vegetative propagation* because it uses the vegetative growth of the parent plant to produce the daughter plant.

Sexual propagation involves fertilisation of female plant parts by male parts to produce seeds or spores from which new plants are grown.

There are many different reasons why we might choose to propagate plants one way rather than another:

—the availability of propagating material (can you get plenty of seed or cuttings?)

—ease of propagation (which technique is the easiest?)

—speed of propagation (which technique produces the new plants quickest?)

—importance of maintaining true characteristics (plants grown from seed can differ from their parent plant in terms of colour, shape, size etc. Asexually propagated plants do not vary in this way).

## SEXUAL PROPAGATION

Following are the most important considerations when attempting to germinate seed or spores.

### Provision of a Correct Environment

Requirements here can vary considerably from plant to plant. Drainage and structure of your propagating mix, amount of watering, temperature and light (or dark) can be important for success. For most seed (but not all), an ideal mix would be 75% coarse propagating sand plus 25% of either peat moss or vermiculite. Most seed is best germinated under glass.

### Pre-germination Treatments

While some seeds will germinate immediately in the correct temperature and

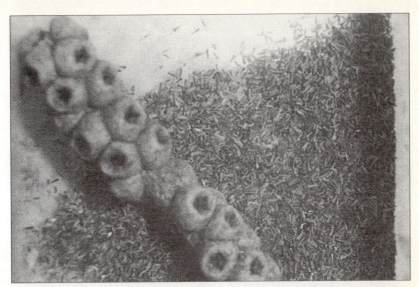

Both callistemon and melaleuca require no pre-germination treatment, but it may be necessary to heat the seed cases gently in an oven before the seed can be extracted.

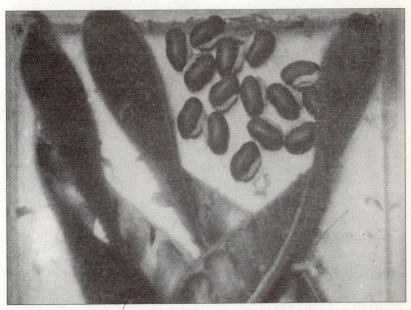

Kennedia, acacia and hardenbergia are legumes with beanlike seeds which require hot-water treatment to stimulate germination.

Seeds from the Proteaceae family (e.g. hakea and banksia) are extracted from woody fruits by placing in a warm position. Fruits then open and drop seeds.

moisture conditions, others have to be treated in some way first. Many Australian natives (and some overseas plants) have extremely hard seed coats which must be broken physically, usually by burning or treatment in hot water. Some plant seeds contain chemicals which inhibit seed germination: these inhibitors must be leached out of the seed before it will grow. Many deciduous trees and conifers will not germinate from seed until the seed has been through a period of coldness. Such seeds are usually stored in the refrigerator for a period before planting.

## Protection From Disease

Plants are most susceptible to disease in the early stages of life. One of the most common causes of failure of seed propagation is attack by fungal disease. These problems are most likely to occur in poorly drained mixes, unclean mixes (keep your propagation area, equipment and soils free of disease), overcrowded seed trays and pots, or badly ventilated areas. These diseases spread very rapidly — they can appear one morning and within the space of one day kill thousands of plants.

# ASEXUAL PROPAGATION

Here are the main methods of asexual propagation.

## Tissue Culture

This is a highly technical method in which microscopic pieces of a plant are cultured or grown under laboratory conditions. Tissue culture allows propagation of very large numbers of plants from one single plant within a relatively short space of time. Because of this advantage tissue culture has become a very important technique in some sections of the nursery industry. Tissue culture requires a much greater degree of expertise than could be presented in this book. If you wish further information on this technique, I suggest you contact your State Department of Agriculture or Primary Industry.

## Runners

A runner is a trailing growth, extending from a plant above the ground, which takes root and produces new plants along its length. Examples of plants that produce runners are strawberry and Chlorophytum (spider plant).

## Suckers

Suckers are growths which spring from the base (below ground) of existing plants. Plants grown from suckers will tend to sucker more than plants of the

The 'piggyback plant' (*Tolmia menziesii*) develops shoots at the base of the leaves and is propagated by cuttings known as 'leaf offset'.

same variety grown by some other technique. Raspberries are grown from suckers because it is desirable to have plants suckering. Poplars, while easy to grow from suckers, are best grown in other ways because suckering trees are undesirable.

## Separation
In this situation, plants naturally produce completely new offspring at the base of existing specimens. Separation simply involves breaking these clumps apart; examples are daffodil, tulip, gladioli, hyacinth and crocus.

## Division
Some plants grow in such a way that *one* individual plant can be cut into sections, and each section will grow as a new plant; examples are phlox, canna, iris, dahlia, and potato.

## Layering
Layering involves promoting the growth of roots on a stem while it is still attached to the parent plant. Once these roots establish, that section of the plant can be cut away and planted as a new plant. The main advantage of layering is that it does not risk the loss of propagating material if the operation is unsuccessful.

## Budding and Grafting
These techniques involve attaching part of one plant onto another plant so that the two will grow together. The end result of budding or grafting is a plant which has one variety for its root system and a different variety for its top. This is a valuable technique in many situations, e.g. growing a variety that is susceptible to root disease on a resistant root system.

## Cuttings
Cutting propagation is by far the most commonly used asexual technique. It involves inserting a section of a plant in a soil mix to promote leaf and root growth.

There are four types of cutting:

STEM CUTTINGS, which use a section of stem with most of the leaves removed.

ROOT CUTTINGS, which use a section of the root.

LEAF CUTTINGS, which use either a whole leaf or section of leaf.

LEAF BUD CUTTINGS, which use one leaf attached to a very small section of stem with a bud.

Techniques of sexual and asexual propagation are covered in detail in Chapters 7 and 8.

# Propagating Structures and Equipment

Two main types of facilities are used in propagating: facilities for initial propagation, which control temperature, light and water conditions to promote seed germination or root formation (e.g. a glasshouse); and facilities for hardening off, which are structures for housing young plants after the initial propagation, providing an environment a little harsher than that used for propagating but more protected than their eventual environment (e.g. a shadehouse).

## COLD FRAMES

In essence, a cold frame is simply a small glasshouse, so small that a person can't get inside it. Cold frames are the simplest and cheapest of all structures. A very basic type can be made by piling bricks one on top of another, to form four walls (a box-type arrangement), 50–100 cm high. A sheet of PVC, fibreglass or glass is placed on top to complete the construction. A wide variety of seed and cuttings can be started in such a simple construction. In my first nursery, I grew around 10,000 plants a year all started in one 2 metres by 1 metre cold frame made this way.

The construction of any cold frame is as above — a box with a top which allows penetration of light. The top should always be a clear material allowing the full spectrum of light to penetrate. Do not use coloured PVC; use only clear or white PVC, fibreglass or polycarbonate for example.

Obvious improvements can be made to any cold frame by making a more solid construction, by insulating the sides (and perhaps underneath) and by hinging the top. Not so obvious improvements are:

—slope the top slightly facing north so that a greater amount of the sun's energy will be caught

—place heating and misting controls inside the frame (see later in this chapter)

—place about 25 cm of coarse sand in the bottom of the frame. The pots of cuttings or seed put into the frame can then be buried, providing partial insulation for the root zone of the developing plants.

Apart from being used alone as a propagating unit, cold frames can also be used:

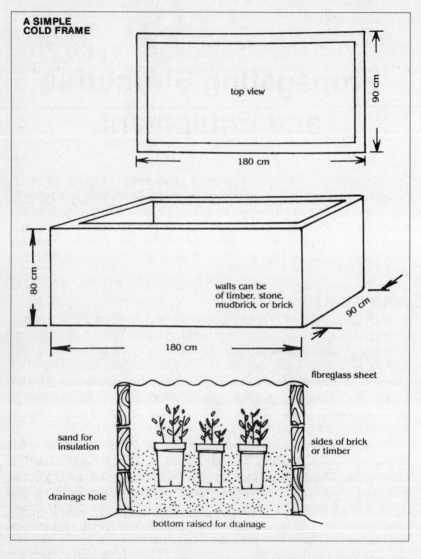

A SIMPLE COLD FRAME

top view

90 cm

180 cm

walls can be of timber, stone, mudbrick, or brick

80 cm

180 cm

90 cm

fibreglass sheet

sand for insulation

sides of brick or timber

drainage hole

bottom raised for drainage

—inside a glasshouse as a method of providing increased environmental control

—as a facility for hardening off plants which have been started in a more pampered glasshouse environment

—if detachable tops are made, they can be replaced with tops made of shadecloth, turning the cold frame into a mini-shadehouse.

# GLASSHOUSES

There is an overwhelming number of possibilities open to anyone planning to use a glasshouse, not the least being to change your mind and not have one at all. While glasshouses are necessary for growing some types of plants in some areas, it is quite possible to operate some types of nurseries without a glasshouse. Consider the alternatives outlined below before deciding on any type of glasshouse.

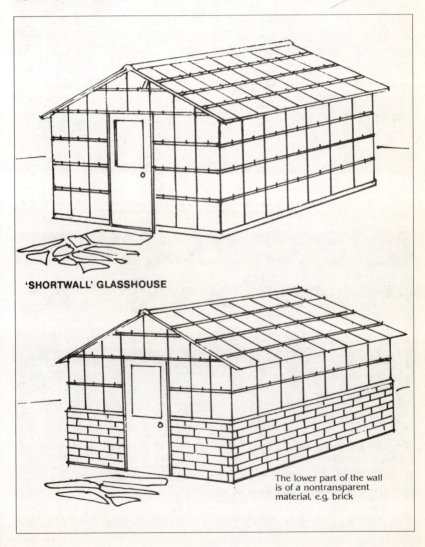

'SHORTWALL' GLASSHOUSE

The lower part of the wall is of a nontransparent material, e.g. brick

This glasshouse, belonging to an established seedling nursery, looks built to last; in fact the construction has proved unsatisfactory, giving rise to wind problems and the trusses have been found to be too weak.

When starting off you may need nothing more elaborate than a home gardener's aluminium-framed kit glasshouse.

# Type of Construction

The simplest is a lean-to, usually situated against a north wall or fence in order to catch maximum light and heat.

The most complex and expensive is an even-span gable-roof building using glass panels in a timber or metal framework. This type of house can either be 'long-wall' (with glass extending to ground level) or 'short-wall' (with bottom half of the wall constructed from a non-transparent material such as cement sheet or brick). Long-wall houses allow greater light penetration, but sometimes retain less heat at night.

Other construction alternatives include uneven-span gable, flat-roofed, single-span sloping roof, geodesic-dome and polythene-film tunnel glasshouses. Of these, the polythene-firm tunnel house has become extremely popular in recent years, particularly for new nurseries, because of its low cost. This structure consists of a metal framework covered by a sheet of polythene. The framework can be used over and over, but the polythene sheet needs to be replaced every two years.

The effects of heavy frosts can be felt a short distance inside the walls of this type of house, thus making it unsuitable, in at least some areas, for growing tropical plants. This problem can be minimised by covering the house with two layers of polythene. The thin layer of air between the sheets greatly improves insulation.

# Wall and Roof Material

Nowadays a wide range of materials can be used for glasshouse construction.

GLASS is very effective, and represents the most permanent of the alternatives. It is expensive, however, and also a little more complicated for the beginner to work with than other materials.

COREFLUTE — also known as 'solar sheet' — consists of two sheets of plastic separated by an air space and bonded by thin plastic strips. It is cheaper than glass but still comparatively expensive; a 15-year lifespan is claimed but remains to be proven. Heat retention is better than other plastics.

FIBREGLASS is more expensive than PVC but has a longer lifespan. Use only clear sheet (not coloured), approx. 2 mm thick — usually sold as 1800 g per m². The main disadvantage is that light transmission decreases with time.

PVC SHEET is excellent in the short term but cracks after 4–5 years (less durable in northern states). The surface tends to collect dust, which reduces light transmission.

POLYTHENE FILM loses more heat at night than alternative materials. Durability is usually no more than two years. Use only ultraviolet-ray-resisting polythene. There is no limitation on size or shape (it can be welded onto sheets of any size).

POLYCARBONATE is a relatively durable, rigid and non flammable material which is generally longer lasting than many other plastic-like materials.

## Floor

For young plants it is essential to provide a clean environment to minimise the likelihood of disease. If the house is to be used for propagation or growing difficult species, the floor should be concrete or some easy-to-clean surface. An acceptable but less desirable alternative is coarse gravel or chipped stone which is free draining, as this allows disease to be washed away. Woodshavings have been used as a floor surface, but unless you are dealing only with hardy species, this is a risk. If plants are on benches, the surfacing is less critical.

This brick and timber shortwall glasshouse features permanent beds with bottom heat and mist sprinklers. With raised beds, a concrete floor is not so important, and timber is a practical alternative.

## Orientation

In the past, glasshouses have been on an east-west orientation, following European practice, but expert opinion has recently suggested north-south *might* be better. No firm recommendation is widely accepted in Australia.

## Ventilation

Plants require fresh air to grow properly. This can be provided in various ways: vents in the lower wall of a short-wall house; vents along the top rim;

windows in the walls; doors; or forced ventilation using fans.

In houses less than three metres wide, vents relying on natural air movement are adequate; above this, forced ventilation is needed. The size of vents required can be calculated thus:

$$\text{Vent area (in m}^2\text{)} = \frac{\text{Glasshouse volume in m}^3}{180}$$

Always locate air inlets in positions away from the plants. Fresh cold air from outside can damage plants.

## Cooling

The growth rate of plants can be reduced by high temperatures as well as low ones. Aim to keep the glasshouse temperature below 30°C.

VENTILATION — opening vents or doors — obviously helps, but is ineffective on a hot day without wind.

SHADING can be achieved by applying whitewash — usually two or three times over the summer months (it is removed in winter). Alternatively, a roll of shadecloth or blinds can be used. Shading helps, but alone is not always enough.

WATER — intermittent sprays of water mist, watering the walls and roof or flooding the floor — will lower the temperature. Be careful not to overwater the plants.

REFRIGERATIVE COOLING is effective but rarely used because of the expense.

EVAPORATIVE COOLING operates by drawing air over a wet pad. The water absorbs the heat from the air. This system is usually controlled by a thermostat.

## Heating

Temperature requirements do vary from species to species but, in general, glasshouse temperatures should be kept between 15°C and 30°C to achieve maximum growth. Never let the temperature drop below 5°C. Various methods of heating can be used.

HOT WATER HEATING SYSTEMS pipe water from a boiler through a series of radiators.

STEAM HEATING is based on the same principle as hot-water heating. It has the advantage of producing steam which can be used also for soil sterilisation.

DUCTED AIR can be adapted to most energy sources; it is expensive but effective.

FAN HEATING consists of an electic heating element built into a casing with a propeller fan blowing air past the element.

KEROSENE BURNERS of the ordinary household type have been used as a cheap and easy-to-set-up form of heating. The main disadvantages are the fumes and the difficulty in controlling temperature changes.

TUBULAR ELECTRIC HEATERS, consisting of 50 mm diameter water-and-acid-proof tubes containing electric heating elements, are suitable for small glasshouses (easily installed and fitted with a thermostat), but are generally not powerful enough to heat larger ones.

Two popular methods of glasshouse heating — electric fan heaters and a kerosene burner. Kerosene is less suitable, though it has economic advantages.

## IRRIGATION

This can be one of the most time-consuming activities in any nursery, both inside and outside the glasshouse.

MANUAL WATERING is extremely labour intensive.

A MANUAL FIXED SYSTEM involves fixed sprinklers which need only to be turned on and off. This reduces the labour requirement greatly, but someone must still be there to turn them on and off. You can't leave the nursery for any length of time!

In an AUTOMATIC FIXED SYSTEM the sprinklers are controlled, usually by some electrical device, so that the watering can take place even if no-one is about. This is expensive, but in the long run saves greatly on time and effort.

This mysterious black box is an automatic on/off control for a misting system. Spray falls on the wire-mesh 'leaf' and weighs it down, which switches off the mister. As it dries the leaf rises, and the spray is switched on again.

## PROPAGATING BEDS

Usually seeds and cuttings are started in a specially constructed bed.Since young plants are more susceptible to disease, this bed should always be the cleanest of all areas in the nursery. The simplest type of propagating bed is a basic cold frame as described earlier in this chapter. Often a cold frame structure inside a glasshouse is used for propagating.

The efficiency of a propagating bed can be increased greatly by introducing misting and/or bottom heat. The principle behind both is the same — that the part of the plant which is warmest tends to grow a little more quickly; therefore, if the top of a cutting can be kept cooler than its base, the cutting is likely to produce roots more quickly.

MISTING involves spraying a fine water mist over the plants at controlled, frequent intervals, cooling the tops of the plants.

BOTTOM HEAT is provided usually by low-voltage electric wire, sometimes by piped hot water or occasionally by mains-connected cables (insulated heating element) running under the pots through sand, perlite or some similar material which is used to fill the bed.

An electrically heated propagation tray with fibreglass lid. By covering with shadecloth it can be used as a mini-shadehouse.

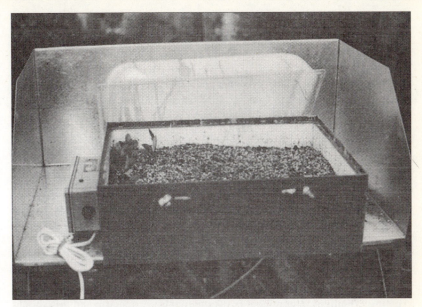

A propagation tray with thermostatically controlled bottom heat.

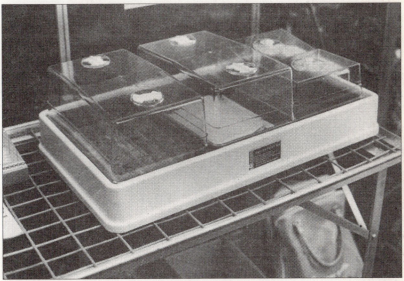

This mini-propagator with bottom heat is the cheapest type available, but it has no thermostat and needs to be checked constantly and switched manually on or off as required. This is a considerable disadvantage.

# SHADEHOUSES

These are used for two purposes: to act as a staging post between the protection of the glasshouse and the full exposure of the open nursery rows, and to protect plants from extreme temperature, light and frost in harsher climates or at certain times of the the year. In some situations, it is a practice to have the house covered with the shade material only at those times of the year when protection is needed most.

Many different materials have been used for shading but today the woven synthetic shadecloth has all but replaced the other alternatives. Brush and hessian shading has the disadvantage of uneven penetration of rain.Rainwater in these houses commonly drains to varying points on the roof, builds up at those points and then produces a stream of running water which washes out the pots below. This undesirable effect is also common with cheaper brands of synthetic cloth. A major disadvantage of hessian is that it will rot.

The other main alternative material is slatting made from timber, plastic or metal strips. These will not rot or wash out the pots underneath but lack the flexibility of being able to be rolled on or off.

When building a shadehouse, be careful about the degree of shade you are creating. The light requirements of some plants are specific and this should be investigated before construction.

# Propagating Materials

## CONTAINERS

Most plants are grown and sold in containers. The exceptions are listed below:

—bulbs, which are sold bare of soil in their dormant season

—deciduous, ornamental and fruit trees which are usually grown in the open ground and dug up bare-rooted in the winter when they are dormant. They are stored at this time in bundles with the roots covered by earth, straw or sawdust to prevent drying out

—herbaceous perennials and herbs grown in the open ground, which are usually dug up in the cooler parts of the year and sold as they are with a ball of soil around the roots, or else potted for sale

—citrus trees which are usually propagated in the open ground but can be dug and either wrapped in a ball of hessian or planted into a container for sale during winter

—conifers, rhododendrons, camellias, azaleas and some other exotic trees and shrubs, which are sometimes grown in the open ground and treated similarly to citrus in preparation for sale

—berry fruit is usually treated similarly to either the deciduous fruit trees or the herbaceous perennials as described above

—some other deciduous plants (e.g. lilac, grapes, weigelia, deciduous viburnum etc.) are often grown similarly to deciduous fruit trees.

There is a wide variety of different containers on the market today for nursery use.

## Standard Plastic Pots

Of all the containers, these come in the largest variety of shapes and sizes and are by far the most widely used. Occasionally a plastic pot will be produced which has insufficient drainage holes, but apart from this odd occurrence, little can be said against this type of container. They are clean, not heavy, can be obtained in a shape to suit most plants and are reusable. Some environment-conscious nurseries have found it worth their while to place a deposit on pots. Believe it or not, customers do return the pots!

Flower and vegetable seedlings are usually grown in the standard sized plastic punnets. Propagation nurseries use 50 mm diameter pots (tubes) for growing seedlings and cuttings prior to sale. Indoor plants are usually sold out of anything from a 100 mm to a 150 mm diameter pot. Shrubs and trees are usually sold from a 125 mm, 150 mm or a 9 litre bucket-sized pot. Herbs are most frequently sold in approximately 85 mm square pots.

## Clay Pots

The main advantage of these is that they are porous and will drain through the sides as well as the hole in the bottom. In situations where very good drainage is essential, this is a great advantage, but in many cases it can lead to excessive drying out. Clay pots are heavy and therefore make more work. They can, after repeated use, build up toxic levels of salt, and the plants grown in them do have a greater tendency to become potbound.

## Peat Pots

These are small pots, approximately 80 mm in size, pressed into shape from peat. These have the advantage that they can be planted straight into the soil or the next-sized pot without removing the plant from the peat pot. They are reusable.

## Growool

Also known as rockwool, these are blocks of insulation-like material, manufactured by Bradford Insulation, which are used for striking cuttings. Growool is becoming very popular in the industry and is well worth considering.

The compact discs are of dried peat wrapped in netting; when soaked in water they swell to form convenient 'pots'. They are ideal for starting seeds, and can be planted out, thus not disturbing the seedling's root system.

Ceramic pots are expensive, but can greatly enhance the chances of selling a plant such as these natives, particularly as a gift item.

Because they are cheap, durable, and available in many sizes, plastic pots have dominated the nursery scene for many years now.

## Metal Containers

For many years, recycled jam tins were used widely but now, mainly because of market demands, they are very rarely used. Many retail nurseries refuse to buy plants grown in tins. Other types of metal containers (usually aluminium) are used occasionally.

## Polythene Bags

In the early 1970s, several nurseries in Australia began using polythene bags, but mainly because they were difficult to carry, harder to pot into and more likely to tip over, most nurseries have now rejected bags. The principle advantage of bags is that they are much cheaper than many of the alternatives.

## Wood Veneer Tubes

These are occasionally used as an alternative to the 50 mm plastic tube, particularly in government nurseries. They consist of a roll of wood veneer secured by a rubber band.

## POTTING MIXTURES

A potting soil needs to provide the plant with the following:
—sufficient nutrients for it to grow
—sufficient (but not too much) water
—adequate aeration (plant roots need air as well as water)
—proper support so that it will stand up and be held firm
—a clean, disease-free environment.

Potting soils are normally a combination of several different components each by way of its own characteristics modifying the mix to bring it closer to the ideal.

The main concern, when considering components for a potting mix, is the water-holding characteristics of the alternatives. If one component holds water very well, then a component which drains freely is added to create balance. Most potting soils are mixes of these two types of materials, e.g. coarse sand for drainage mixed with pine bark, lignite, peat or vermiculite to hold moisture.

Several recommended mixes have been set down over the years but because of the continually changing supply of components and, for that matter, the changing nature of components (i.e. mountain soil from one supplier can be a rich loam whereas from another it can be almost clay), the successful nursery owner continually needs to watch, modify and sometimes change his soil mixes. It should be noted that the ideal potting mix varies considerably according to the plant being grown. If a nursery specialises in one type of plant, it should be able to use one single soil mix, but if a wide variety of different types of plants are grown, three or four different mixes might be required.

A clean, disease-free soil (sterile soil or growing media) is an accepted necessity in the modern nursery industry. This is achieved in one of two ways: either by using soil-less components or by sterilising the soil mix once it is made up. Soil-less components include peat, lignite, coarse washed sand, scoria, vermiculite, perlite and pine bark. All of these are either man-made or else come from parts of the earth where disease organisms and weed seeds are not as common. This means the nursery owner is far less likely to lose plants through disease, and the plants are less likely to be overtaken by weeds in the container. If any soil is used in a mix, it is essential that it be sterilised.

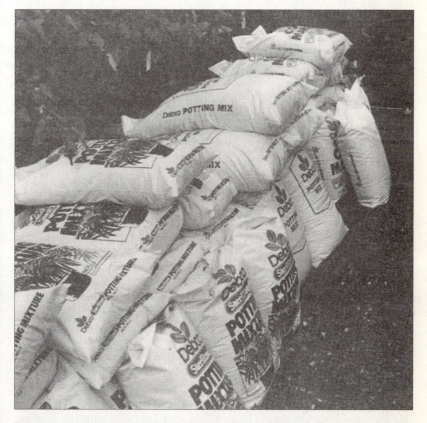

Proprietary potting mixes are convenient, but their quality can vary from batch to batch. To avoid this problem most nurseries have mixes made up to their requirements at a sand/soils screening yard. Mixing your own is only practicable for small batches.

Soil is most effectively sterilised in a steam sterilisation unit. These can be purchased but they represent an extremely large initial capital outlay. Potting mix can also be sterilised by solarisation. This involves laying the mix over a clean surface (e.g. concrete) and covering it with a clear plastic sheet for several days. If the sun's rays can heat the mix to a high enough temperature, most disease organisms will die. Most new or smaller nurseries find it more convenient to purchase 'clean' potting mixes from reputable companies, rather than mixing and sterilising their own.

Another simple low-cost method of sterilising small quantities of soil is to heat it in an oven. The temperature should not exceed 70°C to avoid soil nutrients breaking down. However, the soil should be heated above 60°C to make sure it is properly sterilised.

A final factor which needs to be controlled in any soil mix is the pH (i.e. level of acidity or alkalinity). This is important because some plants will grow successfully only in a certain pH range, and at some pH levels, certain plant nutrients are simply unable to be taken up by the plant.

In general, keep the soil mix at between pH 6.0 and 6.5. It is possible to purchase relatively cheap and simple chemical test kits or electric pH meters to monitor soil pH. By adding lime to a soil, pH can easily be raised, whereas adding organic matter or manure will usually lower pH. The pH is more likely to need raising than lowering.

The materials listed below are the main alternative components used in mixing potting soils.

## Soils

There is a great variation in the characteristics of soils. Often a nursery will be set up in a particular location because of the soil which is readily and cheaply available there. This soil will then form the basis of all soil mixes, other components being imported and added to it to create a mix more in line with what is required. Many Australian soils are naturally low in phosphorus, and thus require the addition of phosphate if non-Australian plants (which are unused to this condition) are to be grown. Be careful of variation in the characteristics of any soil you are using, and be particularly careful of importing diseases with your imported soil.

## Sand

The normal sand used in nursery work is a very coarse granitic sand, the same type as is used in fish aquaria. Be sure your sand is free of any salt or excessive fine particles. It should always be a washed sand. In large quantities, sand has the disadvantage of increasing the weight of the mix. Nevertheless sand of the type described is very widely used in both propagating and potting mixes.

## Peat Moss

Because of increased costs in recent years, this once almost indispensable component of soil mixes has been largely substituted with such things as pine bark and vermiculite, which are cheaper materials having very similar physical properties. The physical properties which are so desirable in all these materials are their ability to hold moisture while not becoming waterlogged, their inability to bind other soil components together while not setting into a hard lump, and their ability to hold nutrients, stopping them from being washed through the pot before they can be used. Peat is light in weight but has a low pH (4.0 – 4.5) which makes it necessary for mixes using peat to be treated with lime.

## Pine Bark

Only a fine grade (6 mm or less) should be used in potting soils. There are two main problems with this material:

Toxicity: fresh pine bark contains compounds toxic to plants, especially young seedlings. The bark should be kept in a moist heap for six to eight weeks before using. Never use if a resinous smell still exists.

Nitrogen Fixation: as the bark is slowly decomposed by bacteria, nitrogen from the potting mix is used by those same bacteria. It is necessary to add additional fertiliser to plants grown in mixes containing pine, particularly in the first few months.

Pine bark is a useful ingredient for potting mixes, but it tends to use up available nitrogen; in addition, it must be used in a fine grade only, and cannot be used fresh because of toxicity.

Scoria is a useful 'soil-less' potting material: it consists of porous volcanic particles having good physical properties but sometimes variable acidity.

## Vermiculite

This is made by heating and thus expanding a type of mica. It can perhaps be described as porous sponge-like particles no more than a few millimetres across. It is very light in weight and has a great ability to absorb water. Never use more than 40 per cent vermiculite in a mix. If you do, its structure will collapse after about twelve months.

## Perlite

This consists of lightweight off-white balls which are of volcanic origin. Perlite has much the same qualities as vermiculite except it has a much lesser ability to hold water. Though it will hold up to four times its own weight in water, it can be used in mixes to improve the drainage significantly.

## Compost

Though variable in its qualities, a good compost can be used as a substitute for peat or pine bark.

## Scoria

This clinker-like cellular lava in a grade of 6mm or less can be used successfully as a good soil or sand substitute. The physical properties of scoria are good but a variable pH poses some problems at times.

## Sawdust

Sawdust and woodshavings have been used in potting mixes as a peat substitute. Their physical properties are excellent but they have the same toxin and nitrogen-fixation problems as pine bark. Sawdust should be limed and kept moist for a couple of months before using. Use 3 kg of ground limestone per cubic metre.

## Lignite

Sold in Victoria as Ligna Peat, this by-product of coal mines is a good substitute for soil or peat. It has a greater water-holding capacity than peat and should be used in lesser proportions than peat to achieve the same effect. It is best used in proportions not greater than 20 per cent.

## Recommended Mixes

The mixes listed below are meant as a guide. There are other mixes which will be just as good, if not better, for your situation. It is best to design your own soil mix to suit what you are growing, where you are growing it and what components are most readily and economically available in your area.

**For propagation of seed and cuttings**

| | |
|---|---|
| Mix 'A' | 75% coarse granite sand |
| | 25% peat moss (or vermiculite) |
| Mix 'B' | 85% coarse granitic sand |
| | 15% lignite |

**For potting rooted cuttings or seedlings**

| | |
|---|---|
| Soil Mix: | 40% coarse granitic sand |
| | 30% loam soil |
| | 30% peat (or vermiculite, lignite or compost) |
| Soil-less Mix: | 50-60% coarse granitic sand |
| | 10-20% perlite |
| | 15% lignite |
| | 15% vermiculite (or pine bark) |

**For potting into 10-cm or larger containers**

| | |
|---|---|
| Soil Mix: | 25% coarse granitic sand |
| | 50% loam soil |
| | 25% peat (or vermiculite, lignite or compost) |
| Soil-less Mix: | 30% coarse granitic sand |
| | 20% scoria |
| | 25% lignite |
| | 25% pine bark |

These handwritten stick-in labels are convenient, though occasionally they are replaced in the wrong pot! Both botanical and common names should be shown.

Printed labels cost more, but they save time spent on writing labels by hand. They can carry a great deal of information and unquestionably increase the chances of selling a plant.

## LABELS

Every plant which is to be sold should have its own label. These can be handwritten or printed but remember to be accurate. If uncertain, don't label until you are certain. Printed plastic or card labels can be purchased. There is no doubt that the more elaborate labels with a photograph do help sell the plant, but they are also expensive. Blank plastic or card labels are much cheaper but have to be written on. Stick-in labels sometimes present a problem with people removing them and even placing them in the wrong pots. Tie-on labels do not move this way, but can ringbark a young plant if left on too long.

Printed labels bearing a photograph are probably the most effective type of all.

In addition to labels on individual sale plants,dispay/information labels are used; a single label is placed on a group of plants or an individual plant in a more prominent display section or a display garden.This label aims to interest, inform and sell. Display gardens with labelled plants are becoming more common in all types of nurseries, but particularly native plant and herb nurseries. It is standard practice in most nurseries to place plants which are in flower in a prominent position near the entrance. Clearly labelled (including the price), these plants have a very good chance of selling. Plants which are to be sold should be grouped and ideally laid out in rows, in alphabetical order, and clearly labelled.

These display/information labels should be both more prominent and more informative than labels on individual plants which are to be sold. Be accurate with your labelling — too many nurseries don't realise the serious implications of inaccurate labelling. Remember, plants grow differently in different parts of Australia, even different parts of the same city. These labels should include height, width, flower colour, hardiness and price as well as both the scientific and common names of the plant.

# Plant Health Problems

Health problems are most likely to occur in young plants. The nursery manager or herb grower needs to know three things:
—how to treat plants in order to minimise the likelihood of health problems occurring in the first place
—if a problem does occur, how to recognise and identify it
—how to treat a problem

## DIAGNOSING PROBLEMS

Diagnosing a problem involves being aware of possibilities and systematically eliminating what the problem *is not* until you are left with only one possibility. It is usually easy to get down to a short list of two or three possibilities. If you are still stumped, you can either seek professional advice or, one at a time, treat each of the possibilities on the short list until something works.

### Parasite and Pest Damage

FUNGI. 'Damping off' is a term referring to a broad group of fungal diseases which are common on young plants, particularly seedlings. Damping off is indicated by the plant rotting usually on the stem at a point where it joins the roots, causing the top to collapse as the base disintegrates. Mildews, moulds and rots are all types of fungi.

BACTERIA can cause galls, rots, etc, but these are fairly uncommon in most nursery or herb farm situations.

VIRUS. Viral problems are usually easily identified; they show as one or a combination of the following symptoms:
—malformation or distortion of growth
—variegation or discoloration of leaves
—reduced vigour
—galls (swellings) on the roots.

INSECT DAMAGE is usually relatively obvious; if you look hard enough you can actually see them. Always check behind the leaves and use a magnifying glass; some insects are very small!

These leaves show the signs of leaf-miner damage.

Rosebuds showing the telltale signs of aphis attack

OTHER SMALL ANIMALS. Arthropods such as red spider or millipedes can be seen if you look hard enough around the plants. Snails and slugs can be seen, if not directly, by the slimy trail they leave.

LARGER ANIMALS. Rabbits and possums usually damage plants in a manner which makes it obvious that something large has been involved. Their bite marks are distinctly bigger than those of a caterpillar!

PARASITIC PLANTS AND WEEDS. Although their presence is obvious, their influence is often overlooked.

## Environmental and Nutritional Problems

A wide range of environmental factors can damage or restrict the growth of plants, e.g. frost, wind, low temperature, high temperature, unfavourable light, poor soil structure, too much or too little water and atmospheric impurities.

For good growth, plants require a wide range of different nutrients. Nutrients are divided into major and minor nutrients.

MAJOR NUTRIENTS are required in large quantities by all plants and for that reason are more likely to become depleted, particularly in a situation where plants are grown in the open ground using the same ground over and over again. The five major nutrients are nitrogen, potassium, phosphorus, calcium and magnesium. Nitrogen, phosphorus and potassium are applied more often, because magnesium and calcium tend to occur in most soils in naturally large quantities.

MINOR NUTRIENTS are required by the plants only in very small amounts, but are nevertheless vital to the plant's growth. Scientists do not agree completely on the elements which should be considered on this list, but important minor elements are iron, zinc, manganese, copper, molybdenum, boron, chlorine, cobalt and silicon.

Some of the more likely nutrient deficiencies are described below.

NITROGEN DEFICIENCY shows as yellowing between the veins on the older leaves. This can be induced by excessive soil moisture, in which case the remedy is drying out or improving drainage. If this is not the case, however, nitrogen deficient plants should be fed with a liquid nitrogen fertiliser. This can be made by soaking manure in water for six weeks (be careful it is not too strong though). Alternatively, use a product such as Phostrogen, Aquasol, or Thrive.

POTASSIUM DEFICIENCY shows as a yellowing and later burning at the tips of the leaves, gradually spreading along the edges towards the leaf stalk. It can be cured by feeding with potassium nitrate or wood ash.

IRON DEFICIENCY shows as yellowing between veins on young leaves or equally on all the leaves. This is relatively common with Proteaceae plants (e.g. grevilleas, banksias, proteas and hakeas), citrus, camellias and azaleas. Sprinkle scrapings of iron rust around the base of the plant to remedy.

## General Diagnostic Hints

Whenever examining a sick plant, a number of factors need to be considered:
—is there more than one problem involved? Often if a plant is weak because of some non-parasitic problem, it becomes susceptible to attack by a parasite.

—is the damage or sickness general or isolated to one particular part of the plant? If a plant is burnt on the exposed parts only then it is likely that the burn is caused by some environmental factor.

—consider any dramatic changes which have occurred in recent times in the plant's immediate or more general environment. Has it been a dry, hot, wet or cold season? Has some protective fence been erected or moved in the vicinity of the plant? Was there a wind storm or bad frost recently?

## MINIMISING THE LIKELIHOOD OF PROBLEMS
## The UC System

Work carried out in the early 1950s at the University of California has led to a complete revolution in the approach to disease control in the nursery throughout the entire world. The UC System, as this work has come to be known, is based on stringent preventative measures. At first impressions a UC System nursery might appear to be practising cleanliness on a level not much different from a hospital and this observation is, in many ways, not far wrong. Every effort needs to be made to ensure that disease organisms never get past the front gate of the nursery. The major practices of the UC System are summarised below.

Use a good clean soil mix, either sterilised or from clean soil-less components. Soil should be physically and chemically uniform. It should provide good aeration and drainage but also have the ability to hold enough nutrients and water.

Nutrition levels should be maintained in soil by frequent light feeding rather than occasional heavy feeding.

Use only clean (disease-free) seed, cuttings and other propagating material.

Sterilise all pots, tools, nursery benches etc. before use. This can be done with a disinfectant solution such as Dettol or hypochlorite solution. Some disinfectants have fumes toxic to plants, so beware. Clean and dirty pots should be kept apart.

Remove and burn diseased plants as soon as they are detected. Segregate propagation areas from the rest of the nursery and allow no-one but those necessary into them.

Have a shallow tray with disinfectant solution at the entrance to propagating areas. When entering, workers should step in the solution to eliminate any disease on their boots.

Workers should always wash their hands before commencing work, particularly when propagating.

Avoid splashing water around. This can wash disease from one place to another.

Hang hose nozzles on hooks, do not let them lie on the floor or the ground.

*Do not under-rate the importance of these practices.*

This small nursery at the back of an inner-city shop needs more stock and several coats of paint before it reaches the potential its central position indicates.

## Companion Planting

This is the other method of minimising the likelihood of disease. Companion planting is based on the notion that certain plants are of benefit to other plants when planted nearby.

Companion plants work in two ways:

Some repel or kill the disease or problem, usually by way of the chemical nature of something in their leaves, stem or roots. Many of these types of plants need regular brushing to release the essential oil in the foliage if they are to work. If this is the case, they are best planted beside a path where they will constantly be knocked, broken and brushed (e.g. Lad's love repels aphis if brushed regularly). Other companion plants do not need this constant brushing (e.g. garlic planted under peach trees will reduce the likelihood of peach leaf curl. Garlic has a natural fungicide in the roots which, when absorbed into the peach, deters the leaf curl fungus).

Other companion plants attract the problem away from your preferred plant. The classic example of this is nasturtium planted near vegetables. The nasturtium attracts aphis onto itself.

Total control of pest and disease is very unlikely to be achieved by using companion plants alone. Their benefit is that they can reduce the likelihood and quantity of problems to an acceptable level.

Companion planting can be effective in several ways: certain plants may repel pests, others may attract them (away from preferred plants), and some plants simply seem to thrive in proximity to certain others.

Most of the plants in the Lamiaceae family (mints) have a repellent effect on insects if the essential oils are released from their foliage. The *release* of the oils is of prime importance; without it, these plants are attacked by the very insects their oils repel. Lamiaceae plants comprise all of the mints including native mint bush (prostanthera), thyme, rosemary, balm, sage, oregano and marjoram.

Those herb and vegetable plants related to onion (e.g. chives, shallots and garlic) contain a natural fungicide which helps deter fungal problems. To be effective, they must be planted at the roots of the plants to be protected. Onions can also be used as a bait for aphis.

## TREATING A PROBLEM

### Nutritional Deficiencies

These are corrected simply by adding the nutrient which is deficient. In extreme cases, it is important to get the required nutrient into the plant and working quickly. Often this can be done only by using artificial fertilisers.

The classic sign of iron deficiency — yellowing of the younger, upper leaves. (Nitrogen deficiency shows as yellowing of the older, lower leaves.)

## Nutrient Toxicities

These usually show as a burning of the foliage. They can be corrected only by leaching the excess chemical away from the roots through heavy watering.

## Environmental Problems

These are usually not detected until after the damage is done. At this stage all that can be done is to protect the plant from a recurrence of the problem.

## Fungal Problems

Sometimes the plants can be given a chance by reducing the moisture, allowing them to dry out. Garlic spray is a natural fungicide which is relatively effective. In the case of damping off disease in young plants though, it is usually a straight choice between using chemicals such as Fongarid or Mancozeb or else losing the plants. These chemicals are relatively harmless to man and the environment.

## Insect Problems

The most common method of controlling insects is the use of chemical sprays. These vary greatly in both their effect on insects and their effect on man and

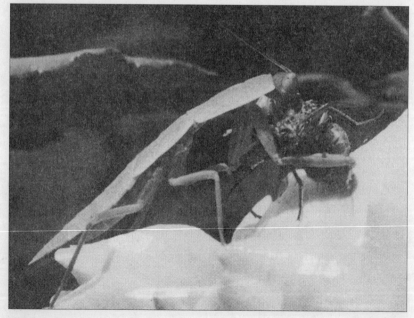

Praying mantis and other predatory insects are a form of natural pest control, but one which is incompatible with spraying.

The ladybird has been a gardener's friend for many centuries because of its fondness for aphis.

Pyrethrum is extracted from a type of chrysanthemum grown in New Guinea, but an effective substitute can be made by boiling the leaves of feverfew (shown above).

the environment. Under no circumstances should you ever use Dieldrin or Aldrin. These chemicals, apart from being very poisonous, remain in an active form in the environment for hundreds of years.

Pyrethrum is a natural insecticide extracted from a type of chrysanthemum. This chemical is effective on most insects provided it is sprayed thoroughly. White oil is another relatively harmless insecticide, used principally for controlling scale. It works by simply covering the insect with a layer of oil and thus suffocating it. Obviously, white oil must be sprayed thoroughly if it is to work.

An alternative to insecticides is to encourage natural control. Birds, praying mantis, ladybirds, spiders etc. will have a natural controlling influence on insect pests. Unfortunately, when you spray insects you also harm these beneficial animals. It is not advisable to mix the two methods. You should either opt for chemicals or for natural control. Chemicals can give you a more effective control, but their use is time-consuming, expensive and potentially dangerous.

## Weed Problems

Perhaps the most important aspect of weed control is never to let them produce seed. One weed can be a problem but when it produces thousands of seeds, that problem is multiplied enormously.

In the open ground, weeds are easily controlled by either cultivation (plan the spacing of your row of plants to fit the width of your rotary hoe) or by mulching or even mowing. In pots, mulching the top of the pot with coarse sand or wood shavings can help reduce the weed problem.

## Snails and Slugs

Stale beer can be used very effectively to control snails and slugs. Cut an opening in the neck of a bottle large enough for these pests to enter. Place beer in the bottle and bury it on its side so the entrance is level with the ground.

## General

A plant is more likely to contract disease when it is already weak through some other problem. Keep your plants well watered and fed, eliminate problems immediately after they arise and your total number of plant problems will be far less.

# Seed Propagation

Although an understanding of the structure and development of a seed is valuable to developing a theoretical understanding of seed propagation, this chapter will largely avoid these areas, giving preference to matters of basic practical concern. These areas can be read up, if you wish in any standard botany textbook.

You should be very aware of the following points:

—seed-grown plants are often different from their parents
—not all plants are grown easily from seed
—often seed must experience a certain set of environmental conditions before it will germinate
—seed and very young seedlings are more susceptible to disease attack or adverse environments than any other type of plant
—seeds have their own store of food to support the new plant in its early stages of life; they don't need fertiliser
—some seeds will store easily while others need very special conditions for storage
—some seeds can be stored viable for many years while others will die if not germinated immediately after they are harvested
—seed varies in size from a fine dust to nuts as large as a football
—some seed can be difficult to remove from the fruit encompassing it
—the germination process can vary in time from a few days to several years, although for most plants it is between one and four weeks.

## COLLECTING AND HANDLING SEED

It is essential that seed be of good quality and from a reliable source. Seed merchants tend to specialise in either annual and vegetable seed or else tree and shrub seed. Very few reliable suppliers sell both. It is strongly advised that you shop around and purchase seed only after receiving recommendations from a couple of the supplier's customers.

It is sometimes worthwhile growing your own seed, but usually only with plants which do not have any complications involved in their seed production.

Similarly it is *sometimes* worthwhile collecting seed from established plants in public gardens, bush areas etc. (For this you may require permission from the appropriate authorities.)

Problems may arise when growing plants from collected seed. These difficulties usually arise through desiccation, disease or cross-pollination.

## Cross-Pollination

Many plants will naturally cross-pollinate with other varieties or even species. Their progeny then contain half the characteristics of the parent plant and half from the wild variety. This problem can be avoided only by growing or selecting seed from plants which are isolated from specimens of closely related plants. Eucalypt seed, for example, is best selected from trees which are in a forest of only the one species of eucalypt. Take the seed from trees in the centre, not on the edge of such a forest. If you wish to grow one type of thyme for seed, grow it in a part of the garden as far as possible away from other varieties of thyme.

## Disease

Many of the legume (pea-like) plants can have their seed eaten by grubs. For such types as hardenbergia, kennedia and acacia you should watch the development of seed pods carefully, removing and burning those attacked as soon as detected.

Lettuce seed is produced in Swan Hill because of its isolation from a virus disease which is carried by the seed to affect new plants.

## Desiccation

Upon reaching maturity, seeds of some plants are immediately released from the fruit. For such plants, the seed collector must watch closely in order to catch the seed before it is lost. As the seeds near maturity, a nylon stocking can be tied over the fruits so that the seeds are released into the stocking when they drop. Other types of bags can be used, but they must be able to 'breathe'. Do not leave the dropped seed for too long in the stocking as it may begin to germinate.

Usually seeds which fall into this category are those which have a shorter life — annuals, herbaceous perennials and short-lived woody plants such as the legumes.

Some plants will not drop their seed at all until the right set of environmental conditions have been met. Most of the Australian Myrtaceae plants fall into this group (e.g. eucalyptus, callistemon, melaleuca and leptospermum). To obtain the seed from the Myrtaceae plants, harvest the nuts, place the nuts on a metal tray and put into the oven at a temperature of no higher than 60°C. The nuts should be checked every ten minutes until they open and release the seed.

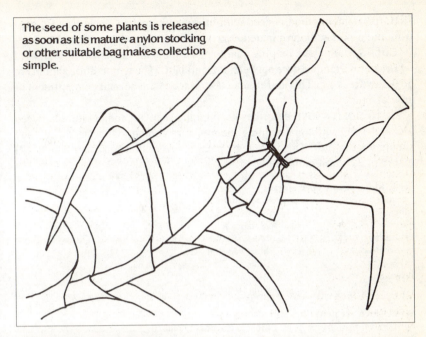

The seed of some plants is released as soon as it is mature; a nylon stocking or other suitable bag makes collection simple.

## Time to Collect Seed

Seed which is held on the plant for years, such as banksia or melaleuca, can be collected at any time of the year. Seed which is released immediately is obviously collected at whatever time it ripens.

Seed from most deciduous plants ripens during the autumn. In the main, it will stay on the plant for anything up to a couple of months following ripening. It can be harvested any time over this period.

Seed from soft fruit (e.g. apples and peaches) or berries (e.g. cotoneaster or crataegus) is ripe when the fruit or berry changes colour (from green to red or yellow in most cases).

## Storing Seed

Different seeds will keep for different periods of time depending on both the type of plant and the way in which the seed is stored. There are many ways of storing seed.

OPEN STORE describes seed stored in bins, sacks or some other type of container in a dry place, but without any artificial control of temperature or moisture. Seed is exposed to the air.

DRY STORE involves keeping seed free of moisture; it is first dried and then placed in either a moisture controlled room or alternatively, sealed containers or packets.

(NB: this same method is used with banksia and hakea seed; usually, seed from older nuts will germinate better.)

COLD STORE — the keeping quality of virtually any seed will be increased by storing at a temperature between 1°C and 10°C. The temperature should not be below freezing. This storage can take place in the normal compartment of any refrigerator.

COLD MOIST STORE describes keeping the seed at a temperature between 0°C and 10°C while maintaining the moisture content of the seed (i.e. they should not dry out). This is done by placing in a sealed container which will maintain a certain moisture level.

**Seeds which can be open stored**

| | |
|---|---|
| Acacia | Kennedia |
| Albizzia | Koelreuteria |
| Callistemon | Melaleuca |
| Elaeagnus | Most herb seed |
| Eucalyptus | Most vegetable seed |
| Grass seed | Rhus |
| Grevillea | Robinia |
| | Tilia (linden) |

**Seeds which are better dry stored**

| | |
|---|---|
| Most annual flower seed | Most herbaceous perennials |
| Most herbs | Most vegetable seed |

**Seeds which should be cold stored**

| | |
|---|---|
| Abies (fir) | Most deciduous trees |
| Acer (maple) | Picea (spruce) |
| Arbutus (Irish strawberry) | Platanus (sycamore) |
| Berberis | Prunus |
| Cercis | Rubus (bramble fruit) |
| Cupressus | Sambacus |
| Fraxinus (ash) | Sorbus |
| Gleditsia | Symphoricarpos |
| Malus (apple) | Vitex |
| Most Conifers | Vitis (grape) |

**Seeds which are best cold, moist stored**

| | |
|---|---|
| Acer | Corylus (filbert) |
| Carya (hickory) | Fagus (beech) |
| Castanea (chestnut) | Juglans (walnut) |
| Citrus | Quercus (oak) |

## Approximate Viability for Various Plants

The plants listed below are grouped according to the length of time their seeds are likely to remain alive and viable. You should note that the viability of a batch of seeds will diminish gradually over a period of years. Usually viability drops at a slow rate at first but after a certain period of time it diminishes quickly, leaving all the seed dead within the space of anything from a couple of weeks to a couple of years. The lists below refer to the time at which this rapid decline in viability begins.

| | |
|---|---|
| 1 year: | sweet corn, onion, parsley, parsnip, delphinium, kochia, acer (some species), alnus, aralia, pawpaw, cedar, cryptomeria, liquidambar, magnolia, mahonia, nandina, persimmon, poplar, rhus, sophora, willow, ulmus (elm). |
| 2 years: | most conifers, beet, capsicum, helichrysum, aster. |
| 3 years: | phlox, verbena, asparagus, bean, celery, carrot, lettuce, pea, spinach, tomato. |
| 4 years: | cabbage, cauliflower, eggplant, okra, pumpkin, radish, turnip, squash, iberis. |
| 5 years: | cucumber, endive, watermelon, alyssum, calendula, chrysanthemum, cosmos, dianthus, poppy, sweet pea, stock, petunia, marigold, nasturtium, pansy, zinnia. |
| More than 10 years | acacia, albizzia, elaeagnus, eucalyptus, melaeuca, callistemon, leptospermum, kennedia, rhus, robinia, tilia. |

Every nursery raising plants from seed needs a variety of growing environments — open ground, cold frame, glasshouse, and shadehouse.

## WHERE TO PLANT

Usually seeds are planted in one of three possible situations.

IN A CONTAINER which is placed under glass (i.e. in a glasshouse or cold frame). Seed sown this way is usually in a very well-drained medium (e.g.

If sown in a cold frame, seedlings are normally planted in a mix having excellent drainage properties, in this case perlite.

75 per cent coarse sand and 25 per cent vermiculite or peat moss).

IN AN OPEN BED there is little or no protection from the natural environment. The ground is prepared by cultivating with either a plough or rotary hoe. Often a quantity of organic manure is turned in at this stage. The cultivated ground is formed into raised beds with approximately one metre between their centres. One row of seed is planted along each of these beds. After germination, any excess seedlings must be thinned out to allow proper space for growth.

IN A PROTECTED BED, the bed is built inside a cold frame or glasshouse, or some protective structure is built over an open bed. A simple example would be four logs laid on the ground over a seed bed with a PVC sheet resting on the top.

Most seed-grown plants can be started in a container under glass. Most deciduous trees, fruit trees and some conifers are sown direct into the open ground. A large degree of success can be achieved by starting some of the native Australian species in a protected outside bed as described above. Many of the perennial flowering plants can also be grown this way.

It is important that during germination, the seed be kept both moist and well drained. For the first few months after germination, it is critical that the young plant be protected from fungal diseases and insect attack.

## PRE-GERMINATION TREATMENTS

Seeds can be classified on the basis of their pre-germination requirements:

—seed which will germinate in the appropriate temperature and moisture conditions *without* any pre-germination treatment (e.g. most vegetables, annual flowers, herbs, eucalyptus, melaleuca, callistemon, leptospermum, etc.)

—seed which has a hard seed coat that is impermeable to water; this must be cracked before the seed will germinate. The seed coat can be cracked by either treating with boiling water, burning or some form of mechanical scarification, such as rubbing between two sheets of sandpaper. Scarification is difficult and can be overdone thereby damaging the seed

—seed with a dormant embryo; this requires chilling before germination will take place

—seed with both a dormant embryo and a hard seed coat

—seed containing chemicals that inhibit germination (e.g. palms); in these cases the chemicals must be leached out before germinating, a process which can lead to spasmodic germination

—seed which is dormant on harvesting but becomes viable after dry storage.

## Hot Water Treatment

Seeds are placed in a jar and four of five times their volume of boiling water is poured onto them. They are then left for anything up to 24 hours standing in the cooling water. Upon removal, they are planted immediately by sprinkling on the surface of the prepared medium and covered with a thin layer of sand (sufficient to barely cover the seed). Many legumes are propagated this way including acacia, kennedia, hardenbergia, pultenaea, indigofera, albizzia and most of the 'brooms'. Usually these seeds are sown in early spring.

Some conifers respond to soaking in *cold* water prior to sowing (i.e. Monterey pine, Douglas fir and Coulters pine).

## Burning Treatment

Seeds are laid out on the medium (in the pot) where they are to be germinated. Dry leaves are soaked in methylated spirits and then spread over the top of the seed in a thin layer just covering the seed. The leaves are then lit. Once the fire goes out, the pot is watered and placed in the propagating area. This treatment has been used on several seeds including protea, hakea, banksia and leucodendron. Many propagators today believe this treatment is not necessary but there is much current research into using smoke for pre-germination.

Burning stimulates the germination of a number of Australian native seeds. Newspaper, dried leaves or other materials may be used.

## Stratification (Moist Chilling)

Seeds are placed in sealed polythene bags along with moist (not saturated) vermiculite. These bags are stored in the normal (not freezing) compartment of the refrigerator for between one and four months, depending on the variety. Most deciduous species, conifers and berries require this type of treatment. Seed is usually removed from the fleshy fruit of berries or soft fruits before stratification. Dry seed should be soaked in water for several hours before stratification. At the end of the stratification requirement, seed may begin to germinate while in storage, so if uncertain of the stratification period required, you should watch the seed carefully. Seed is usually stratified over the winter and sown late winter to early spring.

## Stimulating Germination

Temperature and light controls have been used at times to stimulate better and faster germination. Some seeds will germinate only in a very small temperature range. For most seed, a temperature range of between 15°C and 30°C needs to be maintained during germination. Light exposure will stimulate germination of many of the conifers, vegetables, annual flowers and herbaceous perennial plants including herbs. If the seed is not covered with propagating medium, take care that the seed does not dry out. This really needs to be carried out under a mist system. Chemicals have also been used, at times, to stimulate the germination of seeds. Many fresh harvested seeds benefit from soaking in a solution of potassium nitrate (0.2 per cent). Gibberellic acid and sodium hypochlorite have also been used. Some difficult-to-germinate seeds from Australian and African natives, have been found to germinate easily when exposed to smoke, as they would be in a bushfire.

## HANDLING SEEDLINGS

### Watering

It is essential that the young plants are not over or underwatered. Even if you have automatic controls, it is still advisable to check on watering daily.

### Disease Control

Nothing will put an end to a nursery faster than disease (usually damping off) on seedlings. In most commercial nurseries, a regular spray program has been found to be essential. Though not yet tested fully, garlic spray is an organic alternative which, if sprayed regularly every week or two, might be a viable replacement for conventional products. Several commercially produced garlic sprays are available. (Note; some contain added pesticides such as pyrethrum; alternatively, you can make your own — a recipe is given on p. 120.)

## Thinning

If seed is planted too thickly it does not allow room for proper development of the plants. In some instances, an excessive planting will create a very humid zone at the base of the plants, a condition which is ideal for the development of damping-off diseases. In either situation, you must thin out the seedlings for propagation to be successful.

## Environmental Control

In a cold frame or glasshouse, adequate ventilation and temperature control must be given in the open, drastic changes in environmental conditions should be avoided (e.g. protect during a windstorm or from any late frosts).

## Transplanting

Plants grown from seed in the open ground (not Australian natives) can usually be left for a year or two before transplanting into a container or, in the case of deciduous plants, lifted bare-rooted for sale. This lifting is usually carried out in the cooler months of the year.

Plants germinated in containers are usually transplanted at 13–50 mm in height. With species which have a fibrous root system (most non-Australian plants, many of the herbs, annual and perennial flowers and vegetables), it is unimportant if the tap root is broken at this stage. In the case of plants which

It is important that seedlings are not planted too thickly, because this can encourage disease, especially damping off. The plants shown above are sensibly spaced.

have a deep root system (particularly native trees and larger shrubs), it is essential that the tap root is not broken. Plants with a long tap root should be potted up into a deeper type of pot.

Vegetables and annual seedlings are normally transplanted from the place where they were germinated into punnets with approximately thirteen to fourteen plants per punnet. These are sold as being a dozen plants to the container. In some instances, these seedlings are transplanted into the standard two-compartment seedling box. It is aimed to grow just over one hundred seedlings to the box (fifty per compartment).

Many nurseries transplant seedling trees, shrubs and indoor plants into tubes from the germinating container. Others will place the seedlings straight into the larger sized container in which the plant is to be sold.

## PROPAGATING FERNS

Though some ferns can be propagated by division (e.g. maidenhair) or fronds (e.g. mother spleenwort), most are grown in quantity from spores. The spore cases on the back of fern fronds will appear as small round dots. Usually during autumn or early winter, these spore cases begin to open, releasing the dust-like spores. If you don't wish to collect your own, fern spores can be purchased from most major tree and shrub seed merchants.

It is not difficult to collect your own fern spores. The spore cases appear as black or brown dots on the back of the fronds; the ones shown here have begun to open.

Fern spores can be sown in seedling trays, terracotta pots or plastic pots. Adequate drainage should be ensured. The pot or tray should then be filled with a propagating medium composed of 50 per cent coarse sand and 50 per cent peat moss. It is necessary to wet the peat before mixing the medium. Sprinkle the spores on top and water with a mist sprayer. The container should then be stood in a tray of water; this will ensure it does not dry out. Place a sheet of glass or a piece of plastic held in position by a rubber band on top. This should then be placed in a shaded part of the glasshouse or a shadehouse. Initially, germination will appear as a green mossy growth on the surface; when this has been observed, remove the cover. Eventually small new plants will emerge.

Once fronds are a centimetre or two long, the new plants can be pricked (potted) out into small pots.

# Vegetative Propagation

Vegetative or asexual reproduction involves growing a new plant from a part of the vegetative growth of an existing plant. The new plant will be *exactly* like the parent plant in every way, from flower colour to disease susceptibility. This type of propagation requires that you have a reliable and disease-free source of vegetative material from which to propagate.

## CUTTINGS

Along with seed propagation, cuttings are the most commonly used technique for multiplying plants. There are four different types of cuttings, the most common being stem. The others are leaf, root and leaf bud.

### Root Development

There are three important factors in root formation:

WATER: if the cutting loses too much moisture before the roots form, it will die. For this reason, a humid atmosphere is best, with a minimum amount of leaf exposed to the air and the maximum amount of moisture in the potting medium, giving due consideration to the next factor.

FUNGUS: the unrooted cutting is very susceptible to attack by fungal diseases. A very moist situation or (to a lesser extent) a warm situation will increase likelihood of fungal attack. This problem can be minimised with the use of chemicals and ensuring sufficient ventilation.

TIME: the greater the time taken for the roots to form, the more likely that problems will be encountered with drying or fungal attack. Bottom heat reduces the time for a cutting to establish. Top misting reduces the time for root formation as well as increasing the humidity, thus reducing the likelihood of drying.

Chemical hormones are used widely to increase both the percentage of cuttings which strike as well as the rate at which they strike. The most commonly used hormones are IBA (indole butyric acid) in liquid form or a powder form of IBA (e.g. Seradix). Cuttings are dipped in these chemicals before putting in the pot. An improvement in the strike rate of up to 30 per cent is not uncommon after using these hormones.

Basal wounding is the removal of a thin strip of bark from a cutting. The area thus exposed should be slightly less than half its own length from the cutting's base. This can be beneficial on some species, e.g. juniperus and rhododendron.

Light is not important for hardwood cuttings, since they depend on stored carbohydrates for food, but is important to the success of any leafy cuttings (i.e. anything which has some leaf on it).

Sometimes cuttings form a large callus or swelling at the base without producing roots. If this happens, the callus should be nipped with a sharp knife or razor blade and replanted. Following this, roots should form from the cut.

It is important with most cuttings to plant them with the same polarity they had on the plant — i.e. do not put a cutting in upside down.

## Stem Cuttings

Stem cuttings are divided into four groups: hardwood, semi-hardwood, softwood and herbaceous. A stem cutting is simply a segment of shoot or stem containing several buds. They should always be prepared so that there is a bud at the bottom and the top of the cutting. Do not have any length of wood at either the bottom below the bud or at the top above the bud. Any cuts made in preparing a cutting should be with very sharp and clean secateurs on an angle to the stem.

HARDWOOD CUTTINGS are taken from a plant when the wood is hard, i.e. in winter. This type of cutting is most common for propagation of deciduous woody plants, though some evergreens (notably many of the conifers) are also propagated in this way. They vary in length from 8–60 cm. Plants grown in this way under glass are usually about 8 cm long, but many deciduous plants which can be grown by placing cuttings straight in an open bed can commonly be 30 cm or more long. Hormones are always used on evergreen cuttings but are not so important on deciduous ones.

SEMI-HARDWOOD CUTTINGS are taken from a plant when the wood is semi-hard and when the growth is slow, usually in late summer or early autumn. Most woody broad-leaved evergreen shrubs can be grown in this way, although there are exceptions. Usually cuttings about 6cm long are taken from young wood. In the past, it was always recommended to take a heel (a piece of older wood at the base of the new wood) but this practice doesn't seem to have any significant value. An increasing number of nurseries are today successfully taking semi-hardwood cuttings from older wood (two or three years old). If mist is being used, remove approximately half the leaves from the cutting. If, however, the cuttings are not going to be struck under a mist system, you need to remove closer to 80 per cent of the leaves to give the

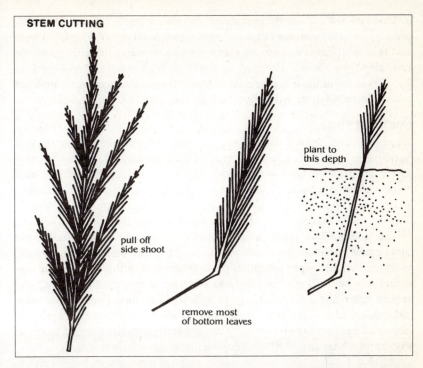

**STEM CUTTING**

pull off
side shoot

remove most
of bottom leaves

plant to
this depth

best chance of success. If the cutting has only a couple of leaves, remove all but the top leaf and cut part of the top leaf off. For most plants, semi-hardwood cuttings will take about 2–3 months in a hot bed under mist before they produce sufficient roots to be potted. Without heat and mist, they will take anything from 3–9 months. Cuttings can be potted straight into the containers from which they are to be sold. After potting outdoor plants they should be kept in a shadehouse or a more protected part of the nursery before being fully exposed to sun, wind and frost.

SOFTWOOD CUTTINGS are taken when the wood is soft during the rapid growth season in spring. Several non-Australian shrubs are grown very well in this way, e.g. lilac, forsythia, magnolia, weigelia and spirea. The type of cutting is very similar in many ways to a semi-hardwood cutting (in size, type of wood and leaves left on), only do not use wood which is too soft and growing too fast. Usually bottom heat is needed to achieve good results, but root formation is usually quicker than with semi-hardwood cuttings. Cuttings are better taken in the cooler part of the day.

HERBACEOUS CUTTINGS are leafy cuttings made using the stems of soft-wooded (herbaceous) plants. Plants that are able to be propagated in this way include cacti and succulents, geraniums, chrysanthemums, coleus, carnations, many of the herbs and many of the flowering perennial plants. Though bottom heat is helpful, most herbaceous cuttings will root well and easily (if a little more slowly) without it. Cuttings are usually approximately 10 cm long with 50–70 per cent of the leaves removed. Most types of herbaceous cuttings can be successfully struck at any time of the year.

## Leaf Cuttings

These consist of either a full leaf or a section of leaf with or without the leaf stalk. In the case of a leaf section, it is essential that the piece of leaf contains part of a major vein, Usually new roots and a shoot will emerge from the base of the leaf cutting, the original leaf eventually dying off. Several tropical and indoor plants can be grown in this way, e.g. begonias, African Violet, gloxinia, piper, pepperomia, sansevieria and bryophyllum.

The section of leaf is planted in a pot of 75 per cent coarse sand and 25 per cent peat or vermiculite so that two-thirds of the leaf is buried. You should be aware that although sometimes the exposed part of the leaf may die, the buried part can still remain alive and give rise to new plants. Misting and bottom heat are a distinct advantage with leaf cuttings. Though able to be taken at any time of the year, usually better results are achieved in spring or summer. Leaf cuttings vary in the time taken until they can be potted, but even with bottom heat and misting, three months is not unreasonable.

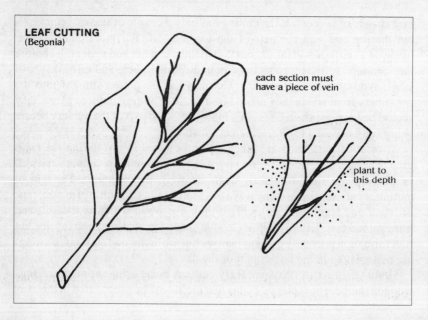

**LEAF CUTTING**
(Begonia)

each section must
have a piece of vein

plant to
this depth

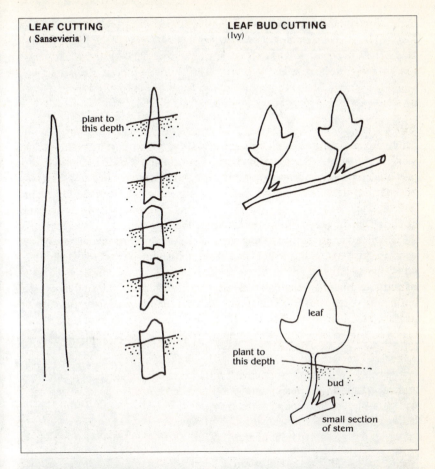

**LEAF CUTTING**
( Sansevieria )

plant to
this depth

**LEAF BUD CUTTING**
(Ivy)

leaf

plant to
this depth

bud

small section
of stem

## Leaf Bud Cuttings

These consist of a single leaf with its stalk plus a small section of the stem (no more than 1.5 cm) to which the leaf is attached. There will always be a bud at the point where the leaf joins the stem. It is from this bud that a shoot emerges to make the top of the new plant. Roots form from the cut surfaces of the stem.

Although most plants which are grown from leaf bud cuttings can be grown very successfully in other ways, this technique is often chosen because it enables a far greater quantity of new plants to be grown from the same amount of cutting material.

Plants which can be grown in this way include camellias, rhododendrons, bramble fruits, ivy, ficus and philodendron.

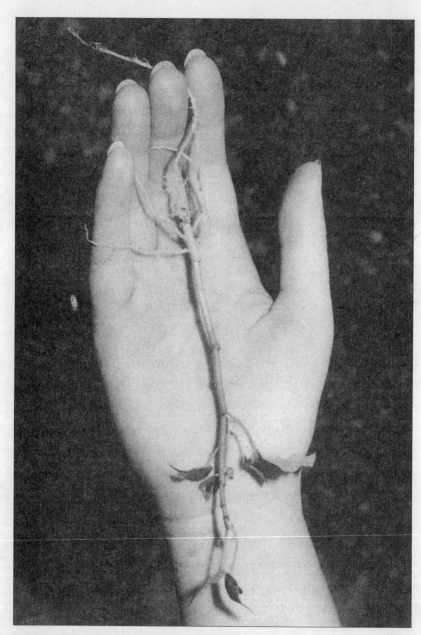

Stem cutting showing healthy root development.

# Root Cuttings

This type of cutting simply involves a short section of root planted in a pot of standard propagating medium so that the end of the root which was closest to the base of the plant is barely breaking the surface of the medium. Root cuttings are normally grown under glass. Obtaining the material to do this type of cutting can be difficult and for that reason, if for no other, very few plants are grown by root cuttings commercially.

The following plants can be grown by root cuttings: *Aralia spinosa*, *Chaenomeles japonica*, *Hydrangea quercifolia*, Malus (apples), Morus (mulberry), phlox, plumbago, rhus (some species), bramble fruits, wisteria and some poplars.

# Rooting Hormones

Virtually all cuttings will benefit from the application of a hormone. The most commonly used hormone is liquid IBA. This is useful because of the flexible way in which it can be applied. The concentration of IBA in water can be varied according to the type of plant being grown and the time of year at which it is being struck. Plants which have a slower metabolism (e.g. conifers) are better dipped in a weaker solution for a longer period of time, whereas plants which grow rapidly are better dipped in stronger solution for a shorter period of time. Softwood cuttings which are growing fast should be treated either for longer period of time or with a stronger concentration of IBA than a slower growing semi-hardwood cutting. Below are listed some recommended treatments which may serve as a guide to hormone use.

| Plant | IBA concentration (ppm) | Time of Dip |
|---|---|---|
| Cupressus | 60 | 24 hrs |
| Metasequoia | 20,000 | 5–10 secs |
| Pinus (difficult) | 4,000 | 20 secs |
| Abelia | 500 | 10 secs |
| Cestrum | 500 | 10 secs |
| Forsythia | 4,000 | 5 secs |
| Sansevieria | 4,000 | 5 secs |
| African violet | 4,000 | 5 secs |
| Rose | 4,000 | 5 secs |
| Grevillea | 4,000 | 5 secs |

# Quantities

It is difficult for the new nursery owner to know just how many cuttings can be taken in a day, how many can be put into one pot and what area is required for propagation. These considerations vary, but the following points may give you some guide in your nursery operations.

Between 40 and 80 stem cuttings are struck in a 12–15 cm diameter pot.

Rose (hardwood) cuttings are planted in the open ground at intervals of 15 cm with 60–90 cm between the rows.

A 2 m by 1 m propagation bed with heating and misting, is adequate for most one-person nurseries. If specialising in cutting propagation, a larger facility may be needed.

The time from beginning propagation until sale of plants can vary greatly according to both the type of plant and the stage at which it is to be sold. Most shrubs grown from seed or cuttings can be ready for sale from a 12–15 cm diameter container within 12 months of starting. To reach the same size, conifers, camellias and rhododendrons can take 18–24 months. Citrus can take up to seven years to grow from the rootstock before the budded tree is saleable.

Depending on the experience of the worker and the type of plant being propagated, between 1,000 and 4,000 cuttings can be taken in an 8-hour day by one person.It is not unreasonable to expect one person to pot up more than 1,000 seedlings or rooted cuttings into 12–15 cm diameter pots in one day.

Usually when the work targets given above are not reached, it is because the worker is spending time doing unnecessary tasks. One example is smoothing out the surface of the soil in pots after potting a cutting, when watering will do this.

## BUDDING AND GRAFTING

Budding and grafting involves joining parts of two or more different plants together in such a way that they will grow together and continue to live as one individual plant. The part which is joined onto the top is called the 'scion'. If there is another part grafted between the stock and scion, this is called the 'interstock'.

The only difference between budding and grafting is in the amount of material attached to the stock. Budding involves cutting out a single bud with a very small amount of wood backing it, then joining this to the stock. Grafting involves attaching a piece of stem containing several buds to the stock.

There are two important factors in ensuring that a bud or graft is successful.

THE CAMBIUMS MUST MATCH. The cambium or growth layer is a thin layer of cells between the bark and the inside wood of a stem. If the cambium of the bud or scion touches the cambium of the stock, then the two are able to grow together.

THE UNION MUST NOT DRY OUT before the bud or scion grows onto the stock. The union (point at which the two are joined) should be sealed, usually with plastic tape, but alternatively with grafting mastic, a material similar to putty.

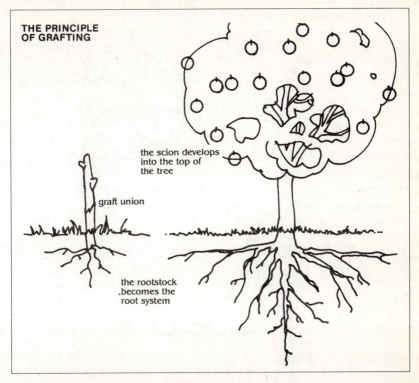

**THE PRINCIPLE OF GRAFTING**

the scion develops into the top of the tree

graft union

the rootstock becomes the root system

Plants are budded or grafted for a number of reasons.

TO MAINTAIN A PARTICULAR VARIETY OF PLANT. It is often possible to grow a species easily from seed or perhaps a less desirable variety of a species from cuttings. The more desirable variety, however, is more difficult or perhaps slower to propagate. You are therefore easily able to start off the particular variety you want. Blue spruce is an example: seedlings will grow well, but only a small proportion will retain the blue foliage into maturity. Grafting pieces from a blue plant onto seedlings will ensure the desired colour in the mature trees.

TO OBTAIN A PARTICULAR PLANT FORM. By grafting particular combinations, it is possible to obtain effects such as the standard rose or weeping cherry.

TO OBTAIN RESISTANCE TO DISEASE OR SOME ENVIRONMENTAL EFFECT. Prostanthera can be grafted onto the roots of westringia to avoid the effects of cinnamon fungus (a disease which attacks plant roots). Westringia is not affected by this disease, but prostanthera is highly susceptible. If peaches are to be planted in areas of bad drainage, they are best grafted onto plum rootstocks. Peaches are very susceptible to waterlogging but plums are not.

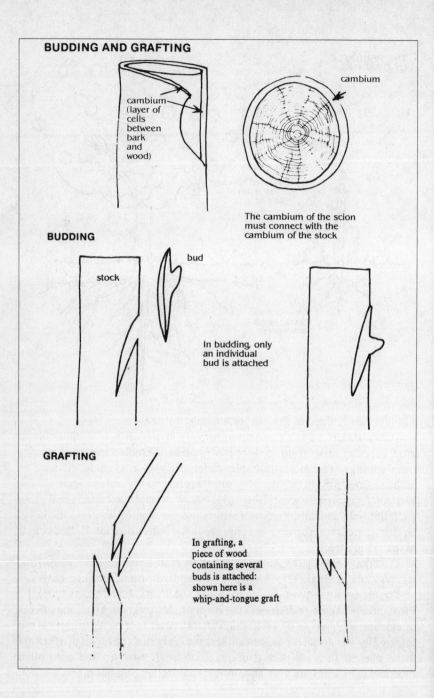

# BUDDING AND GRAFTING

cambium (layer of cells between bark and wood)

cambium

The cambium of the scion must connect with the cambium of the stock

## BUDDING

stock

bud

In budding, only an individual bud is attached

## GRAFTING

In grafting, a piece of wood containing several buds is attached: shown here is a whip-and-tongue graft

**SIDE GRAFT**

scion

stock

front view                    side view

**TOP GRAFT**

scion

stock

Keep scion to one side
to allow the cambiums
to connect

top view

# WHIP-AND-TONGUE GRAFT

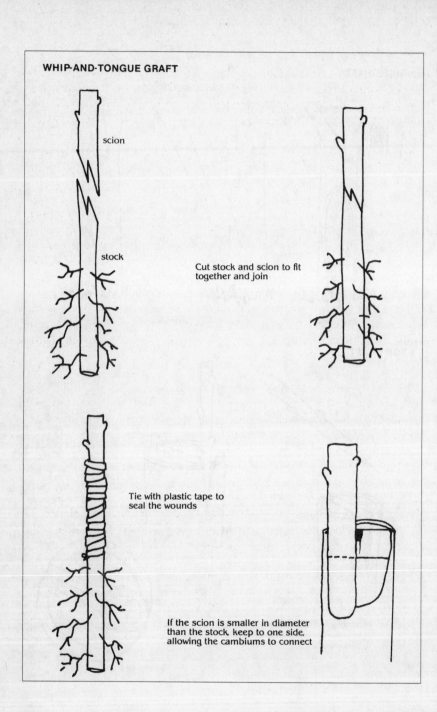

scion

stock

Cut stock and scion to fit together and join

Tie with plastic tape to seal the wounds

If the scion is smaller in diameter than the stock, keep to one side, allowing the cambiums to connect

TO OBTAIN MORE THAN ONE VARIETY ON THE SAME PLANT. It is not impossible to have three of four different apples on the one rootstock, or an almond, apricot and peach all on the same tree. Overall the tree will be no bigger than normal but by using grafting this way, it is possible for the home gardener to avoid having too much fruit one week and then nothing for the rest of the year.

TO DWARF A NORMALLY LARGE PLANT. If a scion from a larger variety is grafted onto the rootstock of a smaller one, a smaller plant of the desired variety is usually obtained.

TO HASTEN FRUITING OR FLOWERING. Many plants can take many years to produce fruit or flowers. Budding or grafting can greatly reduce the time taken before the plant produces.

TO OBTAIN THE BENEFITS OF INTERSTOCKS. Interstocks can be used for many different reasons, including improving disease resistance or cold hardiness; dwarfing or increasing vigour; allowing two incompatible varieties to be joined (if they are both compatible with the interstock).

OTHER USES APART FROM PROPAGATION. Budding and grafting is used by the horticulturalist in other areas than propagation, e.g. repairing damaged plants, changing the variety of an established plant, rejuvenating old plants and in the study of some diseases.

For any budding or grafting operation to be successful, the following conditions must all be met:

—the stock and scion must be compatible; they must come from two plants closely enough related that they are able to grow together
—the cambiums of the scion and stock must be touching
—the operation should be carried out at a time of the year when the stock and scion are in the appropriate physiological condition. Usually plants are budded in early autumn and grafted in late winter or early spring. It is rarely advised that you should bud or graft when the plant is growing rapidly
—the area of the operation should be sealed immediately after joining both to prevent drying out and to hold the scion or bud in position on the stock
—proper aftercare should be given. Shoots coming from the stock below the union should be removed. If growth of the stock plant is left on the plant above where the union is made, this should be cut off as soon as it is certain the bud or graft has been successful. If plastic tape is used to seal the union, this should also be removed as soon as success is certain, otherwise it will choke the plant.

## What Can be Grafted?

The tables show plants that are commonly propagated by grafting in the Australian nursery industry.

## Rootstocks For Fruiting Plants Grown In The Open Ground

| Type of Plant | Rootstock | How to Propagate Stock |
|---|---|---|
| Apple | Northern Spy | Mound or Stool layering |
| | Statesman | Seed |
| | Malling hybris | Mound layering |
| Pear | Keiffer | Seed |
| Plum | Elberta Peach | Seed |
| | Myrobalan Plum | Hardwood cuttings |
| Peach | Elberta Peach | Seed |
| | Myrobalan Plum | Hardwood cuttings |
| Apricot | Elberta Peach | Seed |
| | Myrobalan Plum | Hardwood cuttings |
| | Apricot Seedlings | |
| Nectarine | Elberta Peach | Seed |
| | Myrobalan Plum | Hardwood cuttings |
| Almond | Elberta Peach | Seed |
| | Myrobalan Plum | Cuttings |
| | Chellaston Almond | Seed |
| Cherry | Mazzard | Seed |
| | $F^{12}/_1$ | Stool layering |
| Citrus | Citronelle | Seed |
| | Citrange | Seed |

It is sometimes a difficult matter for the new nursery owner or manager to obtain material to propagate rootstocks.

You can, if nothing else, buy budded or grafted plants and propagate rootstocks from the root system and stump of these. Statesman apples and Keiffer pears are grown and marketed to the public for eating. Though not the most common varieties of apple and pear, with a little hunting they can be found and used as a source of seed. Elberta peach seed is able to be purchased from canneries which use this variety commonly. Myrobalan plum is the cherry plum (green leafed and small red fruit with thorns on older wood) which is often found growing wild along roadsides in old orchard areas. Cuttings can be taken from these trees in winter.

It is more difficult to obtain rootstock material for cherry and citrus. Most nurseries maintain their own source of stock material which was originally obtained from a horticultural research station or from another nursery owner.

# Rootstocks For Ornamental Plants

| Type of Plant | Rootstock | How to Propagate Stock |
|---|---|---|
| Blue spruce | *Picea abies* | Seed, sown spring after stratification. |
| Blue cedar | *Cedrus deodara* seed | |
| Acer | *Acer negundo* | Seed |
| *Agonis flexuosa* variegated | *Agonis flexuosa* seed | |
| Betula | *Betula alba* | Seed |
| Fagus species | Common beech seed | |
| Fraxinus (ash) | *Fraxinus oxycarpa* (Desert ash) | Seed |
| Crab apple | Statesman | Seed |
| | Northern spy | Layering |
| *Prunus amygdalus* | Elberta | Seed |
| *Prunus cerasifera* | Myrobalan plum | Hardwood cuttings |
| *Prunus mume* | Elberta | Seed |
| *Prunus persica* | Elberta | Seed |
| Quercus (oak) | *Quercus robur* | Seed |
| Lilac | *Ligustrum ovalifolium* (Privet) | Seed or cuttings |

## LAYERING

Layering involves developing roots and a stem while the new plant is still attached to its parent. The rooted section can then be cut off to become an independent plant. There are many different techniques of layering as shown in the diagrams. The main advantage of layering is that the established parent plant is able to 'nurse' along the newly developing plant until it is able to support itself. This greatly reduces the risk of failure in propagation. A major disadvantage of layering however, is that generally it is more involved and time consuming than other techniques.

With some plants, layering can be helped along by cutting the layered section, exposing the cambium from which a new root system will develop, or by treating the layer with a hormone such as IBA.

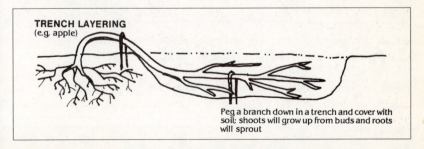

**TRENCH LAYERING** (e.g. apple)

Peg a branch down in a trench and cover with soil; shoots will grow up from buds and roots will sprout

## MOUND LAYERING
(e.g. blackcurrant)

heap soil around shoots in winter; roots will
grow out

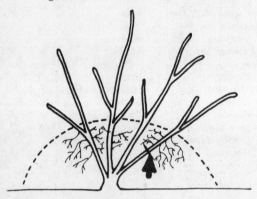

remove rooted
pieces in following
winter

## SIMPLE LAYERING

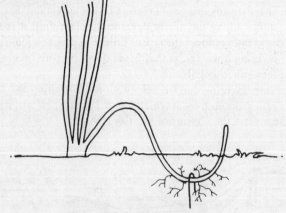

Pull a branch over and peg it under the
ground

## AERIAL LAYERING

 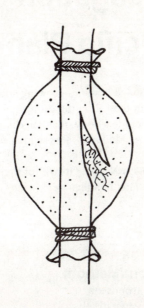 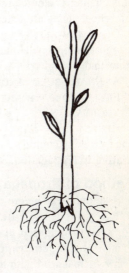

Make a cut in a branch, exposing cambium. Pack moist sphagnum moss inside and around the cut; tie clear plastic sheet around the moss to seal it. After 3-12 months roots will appear in ball of moss. Remove section of stem and plant in soil

# Propagation of Specific Plants

This chapter is a quick reference guide to growing specific plants. For easy reference, plants are listed in the following groups:

ORNAMENTALS. These include woody trees, shrubs, creepers and climbers (tropical, temperate climate and indoor plants) which are grown for purposes other than cropping.

ANNUALS, BULBS AND PERENNIALS. Grown for their flowers.

FRUIT AND NUT PLANTS. This includes trees, vines and berries.

VEGETABLES

HERBS

The following coding system is used in the plant lists to indicate information relating to propagation.

## Method of Propagation (Method)

S – plant can be grown from seed
V– plant can be grown vegetatively

**For seed propagated plants:**

n – no pre-germination treatment required
hw – treat seed with hot water before sowing
b – pre-germination burning often used in the past
st – stratification (cold treatment) required

**For vegetatively propagated plants:**

r – propagated by runners
l – by layering
g – by grafting
x – by cuttings
cr – by root cuttings
cl – by leaf cuttings

y – by suckers
d – by separation or division
b – by budding

cs – by stem cuttings
cx – by leaf bud cuttings

## Where to Propagate (Place)

OG – open ground; protection of a glasshouse or cold frame is not necessary
GL – best under glass (i.e. in a house or frame)
Ghm – heating and misting needed to be sure of good results

## Ease of Propagation (Ease)

E – relatively easy to propagate (this does not mean quick!)

A – average ease; provided you do as is recommended, no great difficulty will be encountered

D – difficult; some degree of skill and perhaps luck is needed

S – results can be spasmodic

# ORNAMENTALS

| Plant | Method | Place | Ease | Other Comments |
|---|---|---|---|---|
| Abelia | Vcs | GL | A | Feb-Apr |
| Abies (Fir) | Sst | OG | A | Use only fresh seed |
| Abutilon | Vcs | GL | A | Feb-March or July-Aug |
| Acacia (Wattle) | Shw | GL | E | Usually Sept. All year OK |
| Acer (Maple) | Sst | OG | A | Best in cooler climates |
|  | Vbg | OG | D | Onto seedling rootstock |
| Achimenes | Vcl,cs | Ghm | A | Spring |
| Adiantum (Maidenhair Fern) | S | Shade | A | Needs very moist, shaded situation |
| Akebia | Vxy | Ghm | A | Autumn |
| Albizzia | Shw | GL | E | All year |
| Alnus (Alder) | Sst | OG | E | Spring |
|  | Vcs | OG | E | Winter |
| Andromeda | Vcs | Ghm | A | Feb-March |
| Anigozanthus | Sb | GL | S | Aug-Sept |
| Anthurium | Sn | Ghm | D | Fresh seed |
|  | Vd | Ghm | A | Early spring |
| Aralia | Sn | Ghm | A |  |
| Arbutus | Sn | GL | A | Sow spring (early) |
| Asparagus Fern | Sn | GL | A | 20°C needed to germinate |
| Aspidistra | Vd | OG/GL | E | Any time |
| Atriplex (Saltbush) | Vcs | GL | E |  |
| Aucuba | Vcs | GL | A | Slow to strike. Feb-March |
| Azalea indica | Vcs | GL | A | Feb-March |
| Azalea mollis | Vcs | GL | A | Winter |
| Bamboo | Vldy | OG | E | Any time |
| Banksia | Sb | GL | A | Needs 15-18°C to |
|  | Vg |  | D | germinate for more difficult species |
| Bauhinia | Vcs | GL | A | Summer; heat and mist useful |
| Beaufortia | Vcs | GL | A | Feb-March |
| Begonia | Vcl | GL/Ghm | A | Any time but can be slow |
| Beloperone (Shrimp) | Vcs | GL | A | Early spring |
| Berberis | Vcs | GL | A | Winter |

| | | | | |
|---|---|---|---|---|
| Betula (Birch) | Sst | OG | A | Winter |
| | Vbg | OG | A | Onto seedling B.alba |
| Blandfordia | Sn | GL | A | |
| | Vd | OG | E | |
| Boronia | Vcs | GL | A | Feb-March. Seedling plants take too long to flower |
| Bougainvillea | Vcs | Ghm | D | Early spring |
| Bouvardia | Vcs | GL | A | Dec-March |
| Brachycome | Vcs | GL/OG | E | Most of the year |
| Brachysema | Vcs | GL | A | Feb-March |
| Brassaia (Umbrella Plant) | Sn | GL | A | |
| Bromelaids | Vyd | GL/OG | E | Any time |
| Browallia | Vcs | GL | A | Autumn |
| Buddleia | Vcs | GL | A | Winter |
| Buxus (Box) | Vcs | GL | A | Autumn; slow |
| Cactus | Vcs Sn | OG/GL | A | Seed little more difficult to start |
| Calceolaria | Vcs | GL | E | Autumn |
| Callistemon | Sn | GL | E | Sept best |
| Calluna | Vcs | GL | A | Spring or autumn |
| | Vd | OG | A | |
| Calodendrum | Vcs | Ghm | A | Summer |
| Camellia | Vcs | Ghm | A | Midsummer-early autumn |
| | Vgl | Ghm | D | Grafted to seedling stock |
| Cassia | Shw | GL | E | Any time but usually spring |
| | Vcs | Ghm | A | Winter |
| Ceanothus | Vcs | GL | A | Feb-March |
| Cedrela | Vcr | GL | A | |
| Cedrus (Cedar) | S Vg | OG | D | Soak seed 3 hrs. in cold water first |
| Cercis | S Vl | GL | A | Needs 13-18°C for germination |
| Ceropegia (Chain of Hearts) | Vcs | GL | E | Anytime; best in warmer months |
| Cestrum | Vcs | GL | A | Autumn and winter |
| Chamaecyparis | Vcs | GL | E-A | Autumn/winter; slow |
| Choisya | Vcs | GL | A | Feb-March |
| Chorizema | Shw | GL | A | |
| | Vcs | Ghm | D | |
| Cinnamomum (Camphor Laurel) | Vcs | Ghm | A | Ideal temp. 27°C |
| Cistus (Rock Rose) | Vcs | GL | A | Feb-March; July-Aug |
| Clematis | Sn Vcs | GL | A | Heating and misting |
| | Vl | OG | A | advantageous |
| Clethra | Vcs | GL | A | Feb-March |
| Clianthus | Shw | GL | A | Cuttings sometimes work |
| Codiaeum (Croton) | Vcs | Ghm | A | Any time |
| Coleus | Vcs | Ghm | A | Spring |
| | Sn | Ghm | S | Late Winter |

| | | | | |
|---|---|---|---|---|
| Convolvulus | Vd | OG | E | Any time |
| Coprosma | Vcs | GL | E | Can be slow; Feb-March; June-July |
| Cordyline | Sn | GL | A | Usually Aug-Sept |
| Cornus (Dogwood) | Vcs | OG | A | Winter |
| | Vlyd | OG | A | |
| Corokia | Vcs | Ghm | A | Autumn |
| Correa | Vcs | GL | A | Feb-March |
| Cortaderia (Pampas) | Sn | GL | A | Needs 13°C to germinate |
| Cotoneaster | Sst | GL | A | |
| Crataegus | Sst | GL | A | |
| | Vbg | OG | A | |
| Crowea | Vcs | GL | A | Feb-March |
| Cryptomeria | Vcs | GL | A | Shade cuttings for first few weeks |
| Cuphea (Cigar Plant) | Vcs | GL | A | Feb-March |
| Cupressus (Cypress) | Sst | OG | A | Spring/late winter |
| | Vcs | GL | A | Winter |
| Cyclamen | Sn | GL | A | Keep seed dark and moist until up |
| Cydonia (Japonica) | Vcs | OG | E | Winter; don't let dry |
| Dacrydium (Huon Pine) | Vcs | GL | A | Feb-March |
| | S | GL | A | Early spring; keep cool |
| Daphne | Vcs | Ghm | A | Dec-Jan; can be slow |
| Darwinia | Vcs | GL | A | Feb-March ideally 10°C |
| Datura | Vcs | Ghm | A | Spring or autumn |
| Deutzia | Vcs | Ghm | A | Summer or winter |
| Dianella (Flax Lily) | Vd | OG | A | Any time |
| | Sn | GL | | Early spring/early autumn |
| Diffenbachia | Vcs | Ghm | D | Spring, 25-30°C |
| Dillwynia | Shw | GL | A | Usually early spring |
| Diosma | Vcs | GL | A | Spring; heat and mist useful |
| Doryanthes | Sn | GL | A | |
| Dracaena | Vcs | Ghm | A | Spring |
| | Sn | Ghm | D | Early spring, 30°C |
| Elaeagnus | Vcs,l | GL | A | Slow |
| Epacris | Vcs | GL | A | Feb-March |
| Erica (Heath) | Vcs | Ghm | A | Spring |
| | Vd | OG | A | Any time provided not too hot |
| Eriostemon | Vcs | GL | A | Feb-March |
| Escallonia | Vcs | GL | A | Feb-March; can be slow |
| Eucalyptus | Sn | GL | A | All year but spring usual |
| Euonymus | Vcs | GL | A | Slow, Feb-March |
| Euphorbia | Vcs | GL | E | Any time. Take care sap is irritant |

| | | | | |
|---|---|---|---|---|
| Felicia (Agathea) | Vcs | GL | E | Most times, usually autumn |
| Ferns | Sn | Shade | AS | Can be slow; keep moist and cool |
| Ficus | | | | |
|   (Rubber Plant) | Vcs | GL | A | Usually heat and mist |
| | Vl,cx | GL | A | worthwhile |
| Forsythia | Vcs | Ghm | A | June-Aug |
| Fraxinus (Ash) | Sst | OG | E | Late winter |
| | Vbg | OG | A-D | Onto seedling stock |
| Fuchsia | Vcs | GL | A | Feb-March; June-July Heat and mist useful |
| Gardenia | Vcs | Ghm | A | Jan-March; can be slow |
| Garrya | | | | |
|   (Catkin Plant) | Vcs | GL | A | Feb-March; slow |
| Ginkgo | Vcs | OG | E | Winter |
| Gompholobium | Vcs | Ghm | A | Feb-March |
| Genista (Broom) | Shw | GL | A | |
| Gordonia | Vcs | GL | A | Heat and mist useful; Feb-March |
| Grevillea | Vcs | GL | A | Cuttings for shrub types Feb-March |
| | Sb | GL | A | Seed for tree trypes |
| Hakea | Sb | GL | A | Slight bottom heat useful |
| Hardenbergia | Shw | GL | E | Early spring |
| Hebe (Veronica) | Vcs | GL | E-A | Most times but usually autumn |
| Hedera (Ivy) | Vcs,cx | GL | A | Most times; without heat and mist can be slow, but still strikes |
| Helichrysum | Vcs | GL | A | Feb-March best but all year OK |
| | Vcs | OG | A | provided cuttings don't dry out |
| Hibbertia | Vcs | GL | A | Any time but usually Feb-March |
| Hibiscus | | | | |
|   (evergreen) | Vcs | GL | A | Feb-March |
| Hibiscus | | | | |
|   (deciduous) | Vcs | GL | A | June-July |
| Hoheria | Vcs | GL | A-D | Feb-March; can be slow |
| Hovea | Shw | GL | A | Cuttings can work under mist |
| Hoya | Vcs,cx | Ghm | D | Slow at times; 25-30°C |
| Hydrangea | Vcs | OG/GL | E | All year |
| Hypericum | Vcs | GL | A | Autumn |
| Indigofera | Shw | GL | A | Any time, best early spring |
| Jacaranda | Vcs | Ghm | A | Feb-March |
| Jasminum | | | | |
|   (Jasmine) | Vcs | GL | A | Most times; heat and mist useful |
| Juniperus | | | | |
|   (Juniper) | Vcs | GL | A | Winter or Feb-March; 15 C; slow sometimes |
| Kennedya | Shw | GL | E | Insects often damage seeds |
|   (Coral Pea) | | | | |

| | | | | |
|---|---|---|---|---|
| Kerria | Vcs | Ghm | A | Feb-March; July |
| Laburnum | Shw | OG | A | |
| | Vg | OG | A | |
| Lagerstroemia (Crepe Myrtle) | Vccs | GL | A | Feb-March; June-July |
| Lagunaria | Sn | GL | A | Usually early spring |
| Lantana | Vcs | GL | E | Most times, usually Feb-March |
| Leonotis | Vcs | GL | A | Feb-March |
| Leptospermum | Vcs | GL | A | Most of the year, best autumn |
| | Sn | GL | A | Usually spring |
| Leschenaultia | Vcs | GL | E | Any time; slower in cooler months |
| Leucodendron | Sb | GL | D | Usually early spring |
| Ligustrum (Privet) | Vcs,g | GL | E-A | Variegated forms sometimes grafted |
| Lippia | Vcs | Ghm | A | Spring |
| Liquidambar | Sst | OG | A | Seed does not keep long |
| | Vcr | GL | A | |
| Liriodendron | Sst | OG | A | Winter; seed is main method |
| | Vcs,cr | GL | A | Summer |
| Lonicera (Honeysuckle) | Vcs | GL | A | Feb-March |
| Lotus | Vcs | GL | E | All year |
| Luculia | Vcs | Ghm | A | Summer |
| Magnolia (evergreen) | Vcs | GL | A | Feb-March |
| | Vl | OG | A | Spring - most times |
| Magnolia (deciduous) | Vcs | GL | A | Winter |
| | Vl | OG | A | Most times |
| Mahonia | Vcs | Ghm | A | Feb-March |
| Maranta | Vd | GL | E | |
| Melaleuca | Sn | GL | A | Any time |
| Melia | Sst | OG/GL | A | Winter |
| | Vcs | OG/GL | A | Winter |
| Metrosideros | Vcs | Ghm | A | December |
| Monstera | Sn | Ghm | A | Spring - don't let seed dry |
| | Vcs | Ghm | A | Most times; best in warmer months |
| Myrtus (Myrtle) | Vcs | GL | A | Can be slow, faster with heat |
| Nandina (False Bamboo) | Vcs | GL | S | Summer; usually slow |
| Nerium (Orleander) | Vcs | GL | A | Feb-March |
| Olearia | Vcs | GL | A | Feb-March |
| Orchids | Vd | GL | A-D | Varies through varieties |
| Palms | Sn | GL | S | Any time; very irregular - out of the same batch some take a few months and others several years |
| Pandorea | Vcs | GL | A | Feb-March |

| | | | | |
|---|---|---|---|---|
| Passiflora | Sn | GL | E | Any time |
| Peperomia | Vd,cx | Ghm | A | Spring |
| Philadelphus | Vcs | GL | A | Feb-March |
| Philodendron | Vcs,l | Ghm | A | Spring |
| | Vcx | | | |
| Photinia | Vcs | GL | A | Any time; can be slow |
| Picea (Spruce) | Sst | GL/OG | A | Winter (late) |
| | Vg | OG | D | Blue spruce grafted on seedlings |
| Pieris | S Vl | GL | A-D | |
| Pimelea | Vcs | GL | A | Feb-March |
| Pinus (Pine) | Sst | GL | A | Late winter |
| Piper | Vcs | Ghm | A-D | Autumn; not too much water at first |
| Pittosporum | Sn | GL | A | Any time |
| | Vcs | Ghm | A | Feb-March; can be slow |
| Platanus (Plane) | Vcs | OG | E | Winter |
| Plumaria (Frangipani) | Vcs | Ghm | A | Spring, 18-25°C |
| Plumbago (Leadwort) | Vcs | GL | A | Feb-March; June-Aug |
| Populus | Vbg,cs | OG | A | winter - cuttings; sucker grown plants tend to sucker excessively |
| Prostanthera | Vcs | GL | A | Feb-March |
| Protea | Sb | GL | SD | Early spring |
| Prunus | Vbg | OG | A-D | Rootstock varieties from both hardwood cuttings and seed (st) |
| Pultenea | Shw | GL | A | |
| | Vcs | Ghm | A | Spring |
| Pyracantha | Sst | GL | A | |
| Quercus (Oak) | Sst | OG | A | Seedlings usually for |
| | Vbg | OG | A-D | rootstocks; sown winter |
| Ravenala (Traveller's Palm) | Vy | OG | A | Any time |
| Rhaphiolepis | Vcs | Ghm | A | Feb-March |
| Rhododendron | Vcs | Ghm | A-D | Feb-March |
| Rhus | Vcs,cr | GL | A | Autumn; can be slow |
| | Vbg | | | |
| Robinia | Shw | GL | E | Usually Sept; all year OK |
| Rosa (Rose) | Vbg | OG | A | Rootstocks from cuttings of vigorous varieties in winter |
| Saintpaulia (African Violet) | Vcl | Ghm | A-D | Spring |
| Salix (Willow) | Vcs | OG | E | |
| Salvia | Vcs | GL | E-A | Autumn and winter |
| Sansevieria | Vcl | Ghm | A | Spring; be careful not to overwater |
| Sequoia (Redwood) | Sst | OG | A | Winter |
| Sollya | Vcs | Ghm | A | Feb-March |
| Spirea | Vcs | GL | A | Feb-March; June-July |

| | | | | |
|---|---|---|---|---|
| Stenocarpus | Sb | GL | A-D | Early spring |
| Swainsonia | S | GL | A | Soak seed 1 hr in tepid water |
| Syringa (Lilac) | Vbg | OG | A | On privet rootstock |
| Tramarix (Tamarisk) | Vcs | OG | E | Winter |
| Taxus (Yew) | Vcs | GL | A | Winter; usually slow |
| Telopea (Waratah) | Sb | GL | A-D | Usually spring |
| Tetrapanax (Rice Paper Tree) | Vcs | GL | A | Mid-spring |
| Thryptomene | Vcs | GL | A | Feb-March |
| Thuja | Vcs | GL | A | Winter; can be slow |
| Tilia (Linden) | Sn Vbg | GL | A | |
| Tristania | Sn | GL | A | Any time but usually early spring |
| Ulmus (ELm) | Sst | OG | A | |
| | Vbg | OG | A-D | Some species put on seedling stock |
| Verbena | Vcs | GL | A | Autumn or winter |
| Viburnum | Vcs | GL | A | Autumn or winter; heat and mist are worthwhile |
| Vitis (Vine) | Vcs | OG | E | |
| Weiglela | Vcs | OG/GL | A | Feb-March; June-July |
| Westringia | Vcs | GL | A | |
| Wisteria | Vcs | Ghm | A-D | summer |
| | Vl | OG/GL | A | Does not transplant well - layer straight into containers |
| Yucca | Vs,cr | OG | A | Root cuttings in spring |

Agave, with its hard-edged appearance contrasts effectively with the softer foliage of most garden plants.

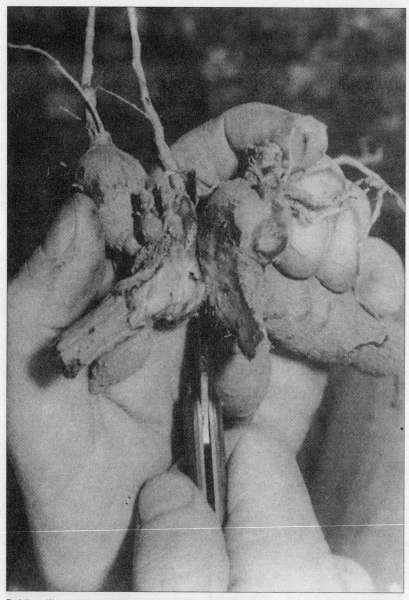

Dahlias, like potatoes, irises and various other plants, can be propagated by division; the tuber is cut into several sections, each of which will produce a new plant.

# ANNUALS, BULBS AND PERENNIALS

| Plant | Method | Place | Ease | Other Comments |
|---|---|---|---|---|
| Agapanthus | Vd | OG | E | Spring |
| Ageratum | Sn | OG/GL | E | 24°C for germination |
| Alyssum | Sn | OG/GL | E | All seasons; warmth speeds germination |
| Althaea (Hollyhock) | Sn | GL | E | Autumn-spring |
| Amaryllis (Belladonna) | Vd | OG | E | |
| | V | GL | A | Bulb cuttings |
| Anemone | Sn Vd,cr | OG/GL | E-A | |
| Antirrhinum (Snapdragon) | Sn | GL | E-A | Light and mist beneficial |
| Aquilegia (Columbine) | Sn Vd | GL | E-A | Autumn or spring |
| Aster | Sn Vd | GL | E-A | Divide any time; seed better in autumn or spring |
| Arum | Vd | OG | E | Any time |
| Begonia | Sn | GL | E-A | Annual types 20°C |
| Bellis (English Daisy) | Sn | GL | E-A | Autumn-winter |
| | Vd | OG | E | |
| Calendula | Sn | GL/OG | E | Autumn-early spring |
| Calceolaria | Sn Vcs | GL | E-A | Feb-March |
| Campanula | Sn Vd | GL/OG | E-A | Spring and autumn |
| Canna | Vd | OG | E | Any time |
| | S | GL | E | Scarify seed to break coat |
| Carnation | Sn Vcs | GL/Gh | E-A | Any time; virus-free cutting material is essential; also tissue culture |
| Chrysanthemum | Vcs | GL/Gh | E | Aug-Sept from young growth |
| Clivia | Vd | OG | E | July-Sept |
| Colchicum | Sst Vd | OG | E-A | Aug-Sept |
| Cineraria | Sn | GL | E-A | Feb-March |
| Coleus | Sn Vcs | GL | A | July- Aug |
| Convallaria (Lily of the Valley) | Vd | OG | E | August |
| Cosmos | Sn | GL | E | Early spring, 25°C |
| Crocus | Sn Vd | OG/GL | E-A | Seedlings take few years to flower |
| Cyclamen | Sn | GL | A | Keep seed dark and moist until up |
| Dahlia | Sn Vcs | GL | A | Spring; get seedling variation |
| | Vd | OG | E | |
| Delphinium | Sn Vd | OG | E-A | May-Aug |
| | Vcs | GL | E-A | Spring |

| | | | | |
|---|---|---|---|---|
| Dianthus (Pinks) | Sn Vd Vcs | OG/GL | E-A | Autumn |
| Digitalis (Foxglove) | Sn | GL | E | Spring; 25°C; responds to light |
| Dierama (Sparaxis) | Sn Vd | GL | E-A | Seed easier than division; spring |
| Echinops | Sn Vcr | GL | E-A | Autumn |
| | Vd | OG | E | Spring |
| Filipendula | Vd | OG | E | May-Sept |
| Freesia | Sn | OG | E-A | 12°C for germination |
| | Vd | OG | E | |
| Gazania | Vcs Sn | GL | E | Feb-March usual but any time OK |
| Geranium | Vcs | GL | E | Any time |
| Gerbera | Vcs | GL | A | Spring/summer |
| | Sn | GL | A | Dec-Jan; use very fresh seed |
| Geum | Sn Vd | OG/GL | E-A | Seed needs 25°C |
| Gladiolus | Vd | OG | E | Corms can also be cut in pieces each containing an eye |
| Gypsophila | Vcs | GL | A | Spring |
| | Sn | GL | E-A | Spring or autumn |
| Helianthus (Sunflower) | Sn | OG | E | Spring |
| Helleborus (Christmas Rose) | Sst | OG | E-A | Spring; seed needs 6 weeks |
| | Vd | OG | E | moist chill |
| Hemerocallis (Day Lily) | Sst | GL/OG | E-A | Seed needs 6 weeks moist chill |
| | Vd | OG | | |
| Hippeastrum | Sn | GL | A | 25°C for germination |
| | Vx | OG | A | Bulb cuttings February |
| Hollyhock | Sn | GL | E | Autumn-winter |
| Hyacinthus (Hyacinth) | Scoring | GL | E-A | Damaging base of bulb promotes formation of bulblets |
| Iberis | Sn Vd | OG/GL | E-A | Seed under glass 25°C |
| Impatiens (Balsam) | Sn | GL | E | 20°C for germination |
| Ipomea (Morning Glory) | S | GL | E-A | Notch seed coat before planting 25°C |
| Iris | Vd | OG | E | Divide after flowering |
| Kniphofia | Vd | OG | E | Divide after flowering |
| Kochia | Sn | GL | E-A | Winter, avoid frost |
| Lachenalia | Vcl | GL | A | |
| Lilium (Lily) | | GL | E | Takes 2 years to flower |
| | Vcs | GL | E | Scale cuttings |
| | Vd | OG | E | |
| Lobelia | Sn | GL | E-A | Autumn-winter 25°C |
| Lupinus (Lupin) | Sn | GL | E | Sometimes scarify seed, 20°C |
| Mesembryanthe-mum (Pigface) | Sn Vcs | OG/GL | E | |

| | | | | |
|---|---|---|---|---|
| Muscari (Grape Hyacinth) | Vcl,d | OG/GL | E | Cuttings under glass |
| Narcissus (Daffodil) | Vd | OG | E | Bulb cuttings |
| Nemesia | Sn | GL | E-A | Autumn-winter |
| Nerine | Vd | OG | E | |
| Nicotiana (Tobacco) | Sn | GL | E | Aug; plant out after frost |
| Pansy | Sn | GL | E-A | Winter and autumn |
| Paeonia (Peony) | Sst Vd | OG | DS | Protect over winter; seedlings can take 2 years |
| Papaver (Poppy) | Sn | GL | E-A | Any time except midsummer |
| Penstemon | Sn Vcs | GL | A | Summer, spring |
| Petunia | Sn | GL | A | Spring; mix fine seed with sand to spread evenly |
| Phlox | Sn Vcs | GL | E-A | Ripe seed autumn 20°C |
| | Vd | OG | E | |
| Phormium (Flax) | Sn | GL | A | Any time |
| Polyanthus | Sn | GL | A | Sept-Nov |
| Primula (Primrose) | Sn | GL | E-A | 18°C to germinate |
| | Vcs | GL | A | Spring |
| Ranunculus | Sn Vd | OG/GL | E | Winter |
| Rudbeckia | Sn Vd | OG/GL | E | 25°C for seed, autumn-winter |
| Saxifraga | Sn Vdr | OG | E | Fresh seed best |
| Scilla (Squiill) | Vd | OG | E-A | Bulb cuttings |
| Stock | Sn | GL | E-A | Autumn |
| Sparaxis | Sn | OG | E-A | Only fresh seed, December |
| Sprekelia | | OG | A | Bulb cuttings |
| Sweet Pea | Sn | OG | E | Spring-summer |
| Sweet William | Sn | GL/OG | E-A | Spring-summer |
| Stachys (Lamb's Tongue) | Vd | OG | A | |
| Tagates (Marigold) | Sn | OG/GL | E | Spring, 25°C needed |
| Tulip | Vd | OG | A | Needs cold climate |
| Trollius | Sn Vd | OG | E-A | Seed germinates slowly |
| Verbena | Sn Vcs | GL | A | Summer cuttings; seed 25°C |
| Vinca (Periwinkle) | Vcs,d | GL | E | |
| Viola (Violet) | Vd,cs | OG\GL | E | Seed sometimes used |
| Watsonia | Vd | OG | E | |
| Zinnia | Sn | GL | E | Spring |

# FRUIT AND NUT PLANTS

| Plant | Method | Place | Ease | Other Comments |
|---|---|---|---|---|
| Almond | Vbg | OG | A-D | On peach or plum stock |
| Apple | Vbg | OG | A-D | On apple or quice stock |
| Apricot | Vbg | OG | A-D | On peach or plum stock |
| Avocado | Vbg | OG/GL | A-D | Avocado seedling stock; select budwood carefully |
| Banana | Vdy | OG | E-A | Cut into 3-4 kg pieces |
| Blackcurrant | Vcs | OG | E-A | Winter |
| Blueberry | Vcs | Ghm | A | Summer; transplant following spring |
| Bramble Fruit | Vy,l,cs | GL/OG | E-A | |
| Cape Gooseberry | Sn | GL | A | Late winter (avoid frost) |
| Carob (Ceratonia) | S | GL | A | Spring, 30°C, may need some soaking in water |
| Cacao (Cocoa) | S | GL | A | Use only mature seed; prevent drying, 25-30°C for germination |
| Cashew | Sn | OG | E | Sow direct, don't transplant except in very warm climates |
| Castanea (Chestnut) | Vg | OG | A | On seedling stock. Seedling trees take 20 years to bear |
| Cherry | Vbg | OG | A-D | On cherry rootstocks |
| Citrus | Vb | OG | D | On citrus rootstocks |
| | Vcs | Ghm | A | Does not produce such vigorous or reliable plants |
| Coconut | Sn | OG/GL | S | Plant 30 cm apart in bed, stem end of fruit sightly raised; plant with nut still in husk or shell |
| Coffee | Sn | Shade | A | Fresh seed - do not allow to dry! Select seed from good plants |
| Cranberry | Vcs | OG | E-A | Cuttings set in permanent location - not transplanted |
| Currant (black or red) | Vcs | OG | E | Winter; currants need a cold climate to grow well |
| Date Palm | Vsd | OG | D | Grown by offshoots to ensure the sex is know. Be careful not to let roots of off-shoot dry out |
| Feijoa (Pineapple Guava) | Vcs,g | Ghm | A | Grafted to seedlings; cuttings in Feb-March |
| Fig | Vcs | OG | E | Winter |
| Filbert | Sst | OG | A | Seedlings only for rootstocks |
| | Vlbg | OG | A | Layering done on suckers |

| | | | | |
|---|---|---|---|---|
| Gooseberry | Vl | OG | E | Mound layering |
| Grape | Vcs gb | OG | E-A | Cuttings in winter is main method |
| Grapefruit | | | | See Citrus |
| Guava (Psidium) | S Vbg | GL | D | Seedlings very susceptible |
| | Vl (Air) | | | to damping off. Vegetative propagation extremely difficult |
| Hickory (Carya) | Vbg | OG | A-D | Seedling rootstocks. Seed germinated spring - no pretreatment |
| Hazelnut (Corylus) | S Vbg | OG | A | Improved varieties grafted |
| Kiwi Fruit (Chinese Gooseberry) | Vg | OG/G | A-D | On seedling stock to assure knowledge of plant's sex |
| Lemon | | | | See Citrus |
| Loganberry | | | | See Bramble Fruit |
| Loquat | Vbg | OG | A | Loquat seedlings or quince as rootstock |
| Lychee | Vl (Air) | OG | A | Other asexual methods successful. Seedlings take too long to bear |
| Macadamia | Shw | GL | A | Don't crack seed coat! |
| | Vbg,cs | GL/O | D | |
| Mandarin | | | | See Citrus |
| Mango | S | GL | A | Fresh seed, remove endocarp |
| | Vbg | | | before planting. Vegetative |
| | Vcs | | | methods less common |
| Medlar | Sst | OG | A | Seed sown spring |
| | Vbg | OG | A-D | Pear, quince or hawthorn rootstocks |
| Mulberry | Vcs | GL | E-A | Early spring |
| Nectarine | | | | See Peach |
| Olive | Vcs | GL | A | Feb-March or winter cuttings |
| | Vbg | OG | A-D | Seedling rootstocks |
| Orange | | | | See Citrus |
| Papaya | Sn | GL | A | Watch for damping off |
| Passionfruit | Sn | GL | E-A | Sometimes grafted onto fusarium-resistant stock |
| Pawpaw | Sst | OG | A | Early spring; protect from sun; difficult to transplant after first year's growth |
| Peach | Vbg | OG | A-D | On peach or plum rootstock |
| Peanut | Sn | OG | E | Needs warm frost-free climate |
| Pear | Vbg | OG | A-D | On pear or quince rootstock |
| Pecan | Vbg | OG | A-D | On pecan seedlings |
| Persimmon | Vbg | OG | A-D | On seedling stock. Seeds need stratification period |
| Pineapple | Vds | OG | E | Cure and dry for a week or two after division before planting |

| | | | | |
|---|---|---|---|---|
| Pistachio | Vb | OG | A-D | On seedling stock in spring |
| Plum | Vbg | OG | A-D | On plum or peach rootstock |
| Pomegranate | Vcs | Ghm | A | Winter |
| Quince | Vcs | OG | E | Winter |
| Raspberry | | | | See Bramble Fruit |
| Strawberry | Vr | OG | E | Because of disease, they must be controlled and propagated only in a disease-free area |
| Tamarillo (Tree Tomato) | Vcs | OG | E-A | Winter |
| Walnut | Vbg | OG | A-D | On seedlings. Seed needs stratification to germinate |

Sales of nuts are climbing as high-fibre diets become popular. The nuts pictured clockwise from the left are almonds, walnuts, hazelnuts, cashews and pecans. All are easy to grow.

# VEGETABLES

Vegetables are all grown from seed, even though some will grow by other methods. It is most important with vegetables to use good seed. Viability of some vegetable seeds will deteriorate rapidly after one year. With some types of vegetable (e.g. cabbage and lettuce) it is extremely important to plant varieties at the appropriate time of the year. A variety planted outside of the recommended time might germinate but, at the very least, will not be nearly so productive. Some vegetables do not transplant readily (most root crops, eggplant, peas and beans etc.) and are therefore unsuited to container growing in a nursery.

Some of the less straightforward considerations in vegetable propagation are outlined below.

ARTICHOKE (GLOBE). Suckers from old plants can be transplanted in early spring when about 23 cm high. Seedlings can be transplanted easily.

ARTICHOKE (JERUSALEM). Tubers can be divided in July. Keep a minimum number of eyes or buds on each tuber.

ASPARAGUS. Grow by seed or dividing the crowns in winter.

BEETROOT. One of the few root crops which will transplant.

BRASSICAS. Cabbage, cauliflower, broccoli and sprouts will transplant but should be planted at the correct time of year for a variety to grow well.

CELERY. Germination can be helped by soaking the seeds first in water for a few hours.

EGGPLANT. Does not transplant easily. Avoid frosts.

ONIONS. Early white varieties can be grown in autumn-winter as a bulb type or spring-summer as a spring onion.

TOMATOES. Main consideration is to avoid frost.

# HERBS

| Plant | Method | Place | Ease | Other Comments |
|---|---|---|---|---|
| Agrimony | Sn | GL | E | Shade seedlings |
| Aloe | Sn | GL | E-A | 21°C required for germination |
| Angelica | Sn | GL | E-A | Fresh seed essential; only a few days old |
| Anise | Sn | GL | E | Spring |
| Apple Mint | Vxyd | OG | E | All year but winter better |
| Balm | Sn Vd | OG/GL | E | Spring |
| Basil | Sn | GL | E | 13-15°C for germination. Spring |
| Bay Laurel | Vcs cr | Ghm | A | Can be done without heat and mist but very slow; Feb-March |
| Bergamot | Vd | OG | E | |

| | | | | |
|---|---|---|---|---|
| Borage | Sn Vd | GL | E | Spring |
| Burnet | Sn | GL | E | Spring |
| Camomile | Vd | OG | E | |
| Camphor Laurel | Vcs | Ghm | A | Spring |
| Caraway | Sn | GL | E | Autumn |
| Cardamon | Sn Vd | GL/OG | A | Sow seed in spring; divide in autumn |
| Cayenne | Sn | GL | E | Mid-spring |
| Celeriac | Sn | GL | E | Spring; soak seed in water for two hours |
| Celery Herb | | | | As for celeriac |
| Chives | Sn Vd | OG | E | Spring |
| Chervil | Sn | GL | E | |
| Chicory | Sn | GL | E | Spring |
| Catnip | Sn Vd | GL/OG | E | |
| Cinnamon | Vcs | GL | A | Warm climates only |
| Clarry | Sn Vcs | GL | E | |
| Coleus canis | Vcs | GL | E-A | Very susceptible to damping off |
| Comfrey | Vcr,d | OG | E | |
| Coriander | Sn | GL | E | Spring |
| Corsican Mint | Vd | OG | E | Any time |
| Dandelion | Sn Vd | OG | E | Spring |
| Dill | Sn | GL | E | Spring |
| Fennel | Sn Vd | GL | E | |
| Garlic | Vd | OG | E | |
| Geranium | Vcs | OG/GL | E | Any time |
| Germander | Vcs | GL | E-A | Feb-March |
| | Vd | OG | E | Spring |
| Hemlock (Tsuga) | Vcs | Ghm | A | winter; slow to root |
| Horseradish | Vcr Sn | GL | E | |
| Hyssop | Vcs Sn | GL | E | Likes alkaline conditions |
| | Vd | OG | E | |
| Juniper | Vcs | GL/Ghm | A | Wilnter; can be slow |
| Lad's Love | Vcs | OG/GL | E | OG in winter, GL other times |
| Lavender | Vcs | GL | A | Wilnter or spring |
| Lemon Grass | Vd | OG | E | Needs warmth; avoid frost |
| Lemon Verbena | Vcs | GL | A | Feb-March |
| Lovage | Sn | GL | E | |
| Marigold | Sn | GL | E | Spring |
| Marjoram | Vcs | OG/GL | E | Any time, easier in winter |
| Meadowsweet | Vd | OG | E | Spring |
| Mints | Vd | OG | E | Any time |
| | Vcs | GL | E | Any time |
| Mugwort | Vcs | GL | E | Feb-March |
| Nasturtium | Sn | OG | E | Spring |
| Nutmeg | Vcs | Ghm | A | Warmer areas only |
| Oregano | Vd,cs | GL | E | |

| | | | | |
|---|---|---|---|---|
| Parsley | Sn | GL/OG | E | Spring |
| Pennyroyal | Vd | OG | E | Any time |
| | Vcs Sn | GL | E-A | |
| Peppermint | | | | As for mints |
| Pyrethrum | Vcs | GL | E | Spring (early) |
| Rosemary | Vcs | GL | A | Autumn and winter |
| Rue | Sn Vcs, Vcr | GL | E | |
| Sage | Vd,cs | GL | E | |
| Savory | Sn | GL | E-A | Seed is slow |
| | Vcs,d | GL | E | Feb-March |
| Spearmint | | | | As for mints |
| Scilla (Squill) | Vd | OG | E | Can be grown from bulb cuttings |
| Tansy | Vd Sn | OG | E | Seed is slower |
| Thyme | Sn | GL | E-A | Spring |
| | Vcs | GL | A | Feb-March |
| | Vdl | OG | E | |
| Wormwood | Sn | GL | E-A | Slow |
| | Vd,cs | GL/OG | E | Division-OG, cuttings-GL |
| Yarrow | Vcr | GL | E-A | |

# Herb Production

A large proportion of herbs fall into one of four different plant families.

LAMIACEAE (MINT FAMILY). This includes balm, basil, catnip, hyssop, lavender, marjoram, all the mints (mentha), oregano, pennyroyal, rosemary, sage, savory and thyme.

APIACEAE (PARSLEY FAMILY). This includes angelica, anise, caraway, dill, fennel and parsley.

ASTERACEAE (DAISY FAMILY). This includes camomile, lad's love, marigold, mugwort, tansy, tarragon, wormwood and yarrow.

LILIACEAE (ONION FAMILY). This includes garlic, chives, shallots and squill.

The leaves of the Lamiaceae herbs are used for culinary purposes, and the oils from this same group tend to have an insect-repellent quality. Usually the seeds of Apiaceae herbs are used for culinary purposes, although in some cases the leaves are important. Leaves and bulbs of most Liliaceae herbs are edible although exceptions such as squill should be noted. In large quantities, squill is poisonous. It is used in cough medicines in minute proportions.

Lavender, a member of the Lamiaceae family, is popular and not difficult to propagate.

Rosemary, a highly prized culinary herb is another representative of the Lamiaceae family.

As its appearance suggests, camomile is a member of the daisy family (Asteraceae); it is used to make a refreshing tea with valuable medicinal properties.

Members of the Apiaceae (parsley family) are characterised by the arrangement of the flowers, which are grouped in umbels.

## HERBAL PRODUCTS

There is an almost endless variety of enterprises open to the herb farm. There is a definite difference between the profitable and the interesting possibilities, and the serious new herb farmers might have to modify their ambitions in order to achieve a profit.

Most business in the herb farm industry involves the following four areas: production and sale of plants, seeds, dried herbs and herbal oils.

There is a market for a wide range of other herbal products but for the moment this market remains relatively small.

Examples are sachets and potpourris, vinegars, bath salts, oils and cosmetics (generally controlled by the large cosmetic companies), pickles, soaps, jams, medicines, insect-repellent sprays, sauces, sleep pillows, tobacco, incense and scented candles.

Many attractive herbal gift items can be produced for sale in the nursery. Their popularity, however, is largely governed by the degree of attention given to their presentation and display. These attractive sachets of potpourri and lavender will be labelled and packed in clear cellophane bags before being placed on sale at the counter of a country herb farm.

## Production and Sale of Plants

Herbs are grown for sale in containers and also in the open ground. Growing and selling in 7 to 15 cm diameter pots is more common, but from the open ground, they can be dug in winter and sold bare with only the soil which clings in a ball to the roots.

Most herbs grow well from both seed and cuttings (refer to propagation charts for details). Several herbs are also easily grown from division. Herbs are a relatively fast-growing group of plants, reaching a saleable size usually within six months of propagation. For this reason, herbs are usually sold at a lower price than woody shrubs and trees. To obtain a reasonable living from a herb nursery a single person would need to produce and sell between 15,000 and 30,000 plants a year. A herb farm usually relies heavily on sales of plants but often supplements this with sales of herbal products, books and general nursery lines.

## Production of Seed

Seed needs to be harvested when it is mature, just prior to dropping. The experienced seed gardener can know the time almost by instinct, but the inexperienced must watch the plants closely. Perhaps the best indication of the seed's approach to maturity is a colour change (usually from a green to a brown or autumn tone). At this stage, a stocking can be tied over the seed head. When the seed drops, it will be caught by the stocking. The experienced person does not need the stocking for most plants.

Seed will keep best if it is stored dry in a sealed container (not vacuum sealed however). The keeping quality of herb seed varies from one year to five years. Most keep at least two years.

If you are growing seed for sale through your own retail outlet (i.e. to the public on the roadside or at the nursery), you will probably obtain sufficient seed from a couple of plants of each variety. If selling to a seed company, you would grow much larger quantities.

## Dried Herbs

Herbs should be dried either indoors or in a specially constructed drying cabinet. It is important that rain does not interrupt the drying process. A herb which half dries, moistens, then continues to dry again, will lose much of its quality. The main requirements are:

—a fairly constant temperature between 27°C and 32°C (for most — but not all)

—good air movement around the herb

—shade for any top growth

—sunlight for drying roots.

Do not dry in any room which might become humid, i.e. a kitchen, bathroom, laundry or a room which has indoor plants. Herbs should be dried immediately after they are harvested, either spread out on wire mesh shelves or hung upside down so that air can move freely around all parts of the plant. It helps to turn the plants every day or so until dry. When the plant parts will break easily without bending or with little pressure, then they are sufficiently dry. They are then best stored in a dry airtight container.

## Herbal Oils

These are made by distilling the oil from the plant parts or by steeping the plant parts in a non-aromatic vegetable oil such as sunflower, safflower, peanut or olive oil.

Rose petals, rosemary or lavender can be crushed, then stood in one of these vegetable oils in a sealed jar. If placed in the sun or some other warm position the aroma of the plant will soon penetrate the oil. Use 5g of flowers or foliage to 500 ml of oil. Herb cooking or cleansing oils are made in this way.

Distilled oils of some plants are produced on a larger scale for use in certain industries. Lavender, spearmint, peppermint and eucalyptus oils are among the more obvious ones. *Melaleuca alternifolia* is a native paperbark which provides the well-known tea-tree oil, and which is used in the production of fire gel. This is in high demand worldwide.

## Potpourri

There are two basic methods of making potpourri: the old-fashioned moist method, in which partly dried petals and leaves are mixed with salt and left to mature, and the dry method, which is generally preferred today, and which requires a fixative to preserve the scent.

Here is a typical recipe for the dry method (the leaves and petals should be completely dry):

4 cups rose petals
2 cups scented geranium leaves
2 cups lavender flowers and leaves
1 cup lemon verbena leaves
2 tablespoons orris root powder (fixative)
1 teaspoon rose geranium oil
1 teaspoon lavender oil
1 teaspoon ground cloves
1 teaspoon ground cinnamon
12 whole flowers

Mix the above ingredients together in a glass jar and leave sealed for one month. This mix can then be placed into pomanders. These are containers, often made from cane, with holes in them to allow the aroma to be released.

## Herb Mixes

There are three common mixtures of dried herbs.

BOUQUET GARNI. Parsley, thyme, bay and sometimes others are used. This is hung in muslin bags for the aroma, or used in cooking.

MIXED HERBS. The standard 'mixed herbs' used in cooking are marjoram, thyme and sage.

FINES HERBS. Used in cooking, these include chervil, chives, parsley and tarragon.

## Herb Sprays

In the past, many small herb farms have produced herbal pest sprays to sell either direct from the farm, or through local distributors such as nurseries or tourist shops. A range of safe repellents, insecticides and fungicides can be

Herbal insect repellents and insecticides are becoming increasingly popular among organically minded growers.

made simply and easily from herbs. Be careful how such products are promoted though, because there are laws governing the sale of pesticides and other types of chemicals. Such laws may restrict what can be sold and how it can be labelled in some parts of the world.

GARLIC SPRAY. Pour 10 ml of paraffin oil over 90 g of crushed garlic, cover and allow to stand for 48 hours. Make a soap solution using 10 g of soap in 500 ml of hot water. Pour the soapy water over the garlic and leave covered for one day, then warm the mixture and strain. This can be bottled and should be diluted by adding between 10 and 50 parts of water for spraying.

OTHER SPRAYS. Sprays of sage, wormwood, camomile, stinging nettle and others can be made by placing the fresh leaves in boiling water and leaving to stand. After 24 hours, the tea is strained off and stored in a sealed bottle.

Camomile and garlic sprays will control fungus problems to some extent. Wormwood acts as an insect-repellent spray.

## Herbal Medicine

Many herbs have positive medicinal value, and some (such as peppermint and eucalyptus) are used extensively in traditional medicine. Be careful though, as there are some herbs which have their use based more on tradition or superstition than sound knowledge. It is advised that prior to production of any medicinal herb products, you should carefully check your source of information.

# Setting Up A Commercial Herb Farm

(By Iain Harrison: Senior Tutor Australian Correspondence Schools)

## WHY GROW HERBS COMMERCIALLY?

Without doubt, the prime reason for growing herbs on a commercial basis is that there is a demand worldwide for herbal products, both fresh and processed. It has been estimated that the demand for spices, condiments and similar products is increasing by, in some cases, more than 20% annually (Miller & Harper: Herb Market Report Vol.5, No.11,1989). There is considerable potential to grow herbs as an alternative to existing mainstream crops that are in oversupply. There is not much point in producing a product if there is no demand for it. If there is demand, however, and you can produce goods of consistent quality at a competitive price then you should be able to sell your crop profitably.

Herbs have several other advantages as a commercial crop. Many can be grown in areas with poor soil or limited water supply. Generally much less growing space is required than for more commonly grown crops. The end products are generally small in volume, so storage, packaging, and transport requirements are not usually as high as for other crops. Many herbs also have high pest- and disease-resistance so the use of pesticides can be greatly reduced. There is also considerable potential for value added products, for example herb vinegars or wines, craft items, and cooked herb goods.

## The Possibilities

Herbs can be grown commercially in many different ways, and can be marketed in many different forms. Ways to grow include:

BROADACRE: This can be an excellent way of growing larger sized herbs, or where large quantities of the crop are required. This can happen where there is sufficient demand for large quantities of the fresh crop, or when large quantities of the 'raw' crop are required to provide sufficient quantities after processing of the 'finished' crop, for example, processing of essential oils where oil content may be only 1 or 2% of the raw material. Broadacre cropping of herbs can be a good alternative for established growers who are looking for something new to grow. For new growers this type of growing may be very expensive to set up.

INTENSIVE IN-GROUND CROPPING. This type of cropping is suitable for generally smaller, high yielding crops. Fresh culinary herbs are a good example. This type of cropping will normally be cheaper to establish than broadacre cropping, but will often be quite labour-intensive. This can sometimes be an advantage, in times of high unemployment, as a means of creating gainful, satisfying employment.

HYDROPONICS. Though equipment costs are high initially, the land required is minimal, and yields can be very high from small areas. Pest and disease

Beans, grown here in well-mulched rows which reduce labour cost of weeding.

problems are usually greatly reduced in comparison to in-ground production. Greater technical expertise is required to operate the system in comparison to most in-ground cropping. The crops can be grown at waist, (or other suitable) height, which greatly eases the effort required in planting, maintaining and harvesting the crops.

Hydroponic growing has proven very successful for growing fresh salad vegetables. Fresh culinary herbs are also being successfully grown commercially in Australia, the USA, and several European countries. A well-operated hydroponic system has considerable environmental advantages as well. Nutrient runoff to streams often associated with agricultural production can be controlled or minimised, and as hydroponic growing is 'soil-less', there is greatly reduced demand on our valuable top soils.

CONTAINERS. Herbs can be readily grown in containers of all shapes and sizes. This enables them to be readily moved around as desired. You may decide to grow herbs in pots for sale to nurseries or directly to home growers. You could also include herbs in hanging baskets.

Another way is to grow culinary herbs in lightweight containers such as

Although initially expensive to set up, a greenhouse offers advantages to producers in terms of propagation and establishment of stock early in the growing season or production of plants that may be sensitive to outdoor conditions.

polystyrene fruit boxes which can be easily transported to markets, or even hotels and restaurants, so that the herbs can be harvested fresh from the containers as required. For perennial herbs the containers could even be returned to you to allow the herbs to re-shoot before harvesting again.

GREENHOUSE GROWING. This type of growing is ideal for the production of crops that may be sensitive to outdoor conditions in your area, or for producing increased yields of other crops. The greenhouses can be initially quite expensive to set up and this type of cropping can be quite labour-intensive. It has the advantages that, like hydroponics, the crops can be grown on benches at a comfortable height, and if good hygiene is maintained then pest, disease and weed problems can be minimised. Greenhouses can be also extremely useful for other types of cropping, as a means of propagating your own planting stock, or for getting stock established early.

## Types Of Herb Goods To Produce

The types of goods that can be produced from herbs is virtually endless. They can be grouped into a number of main types. These are:

FRESH: principally for culinary use, sometimes as stock feed.

DRIED: widely used for culinary use, as floral or dried arrangements and for providing fragrance.

PROCESSED: this includes those herbs that have further treatment in some way, for example crushing or powdering. These types are commonly used in medicinals and cosmetics.

ESSENTIAL OILS: these are widely used as medicinals, for aromatherapy, as flavourings or condiments, as pesticides, as fixatives or bases for other ingredients (i.e. in perfumes) and as massage oils.

## HARVESTING YOUR HERBS

Herbs are generally harvested by hand, for those where appearance is important (i.e. fresh, culinary herbs), or by machine, where further processing (i.e. distillation) is to take place. Once harvested, herbs can rapidly decline in appearance and chemical content if not processed in some way to preserve their quality. Deciding on which way to process your product will depend on what type of herbs you are growing, what type of market you are aiming for, and how much you wish to spend on establishing processing and storage facilities.

To get the best from your herbs they should be harvested when they are at their best with regard to appearance (colour, texture, and moisture content or turgor), and at peak concentration of oil and aromatic compounds. There may need to be some compromise between these components as it is rare that they are all at their peak at one time. For example, herbs such as rosemary and lavender, which are to be harvested for their oil and other chemicals, have their peak content of these products just before or during flowering, while culinary herbs can often be harvested throughout the growing season. Ideally harvesting should take place early in the morning to reduce the loss of volatile compounds, and so that the plant material is more easily cooled to the desired storage temperature. Take care to avoid damaging harvested material, as this will result in early deterioration.

## Fresh Herbs

To increase the longevity of fresh herbs they can be refrigerated. Temperatures around 1–5°C will suit most leafy herbs. High humidities of around 90 to 95% in the storage area will help reduce water loss from the harvested material. Plastic wrapping will help maintain humidity levels, but be sure to check regularly for the signs of any rotting occuring. Sealed packaging, soon after harvesting, will also help maintain moisture levels. For the longer term, controlled atmosphere storage can greatly extend the lifespan and maintain the quality of the product. This type of storage can be quite expensive to establish.

## Processed Herbs

There are a number of different processes that can be used to preserve herbs. The most common is drying. On a large scale herbs can be dried in the field. This is very dependent on having good weather conditions, and therefore is only used in areas where weather conditions are consistently good at harvest time and/or other drying methods are prohibitive in cost. For more consistent results, herbs can be dried by laying or hanging them on racks or benches of some type that allows good air circulation. These racks can be roofed to provide weather protection or, in good weather conditions, can be left open. Roll up sides can also be used to provide additional protection.

## Example of a Drying Shed

A large galvanised iron farm or work shed, with a concrete slab base can be purchased for less than $5,000. Such a shed should have large doors to allow good ventilation. Do not include skylights (e.g. fibreglass or similar sheeting) in the shed walls or roof, as herbs will rapidly lose their volatile oils if exposed to light. Racks can be purchased complete or in kit form from a number of suppliers, or you can make them yourself using either metal or treated timber supports and wire mesh racking. This can be done for as little as two or three thousand dollars. Second-hand racking such as those used by dried fruit growers can sometimes be purchased at clearing sales.

For controlled drying, kilns or ovens can be used. These can be initially expensive to set up, but give very good results, depending on the herbs being dried, if operated correctly. For small quantities microwave ovens have

Peppermint, a member of the Lamiaceae family, has a repellent effect on insects if the essential oils are released. These oils can be extracted for use in medicines, aromatherapy and insect-repellent sprays.

shown some promise. Experimentation is the key here to establishing the best temperature and drying times.

Freezing has proven successful for many different herbs. As with frozen vegetables, the herbs can be removed in sections or pieces as required, and either thawed before use or added as is.

Fermentation can also be used for some types of herbs as a means of preserving their properties. This generally requires some degree of technical knowledge. Licences or permits may also be required. Distillation of essential oils is becoming increasingly popular, for example, lavender, rosemary, eucalyptus, and Australian tea-tree. As with fermentation, greater technical knowledge is necessary and permits or licences may be required. The distillation equipment can be expensive to install.

## Chemical Treatments

Chemicals such as fungicides and bactericides are sometimes applied to inhibit or stop microbial growth, and hence reduce deterioration of the harvested material. Chemicals can also be applied to reduce water loss.

## CHOOSING WHAT TO GROW

This is usually the hardest part of growing a new product, choosing the right one! Very few authoritative statistics are kept in most developed nations, including Australia and the USA. It is not clear how much, what types, and at what price herbal products are sold because what we would consider as being herbal products are often listed under another category for 'official statistics', e.g. essential oils may be included under pharmaceuticals. Most writers on the subject agree, however, that there is a consistent increase in annual demand for herbal products in all their forms. This has gained impetus in recent years, as the trend to more natural based products increases.

Determining what to grow therefore involves some detective work on your part. In other words you have to go out and find what the consumers want. This can be done in a number of ways fairly simply, without involving very extensive market research. While extensive statistics are rarely available, it is possible to obtain some that can be very useful. Bureau of Statistics figures for agricultural production will give you some indication of what types of products are being grown already in Australia, while import/export statistics will help you to find out what products are being sold overseas (and where), and which are being imported into the country in large quantities.

State or Regional Departments of Agriculture or Primary Industries can often provide information on which products are in demand, which varieties would be suitable for your area (if you already have a property), where to get good quality varieties, and how to grow them. Trade or specific interest magazines and journals will often have articles on industry trends, or information on new or uncommon varieties to grow. Grower groups can provide advice and a source of planting stock. Telephoning or visiting wholesalers, nurseries, local restaurants, hotels, produce merchants or brokers can give you a good idea of what is in demand and if there is a shortage or oversupply of particular herbal products. Another alternative is to create your own market by growing something that is unusual or new. There is also considerable potential for 'value added' products.

Once you have chosen what variety or type of herb to grow it is then very important that you get the best variety of that herb or herbs for your situation. This can often be very hard to do. Little selection work to choose the best cultivars of herbs has been carried out, as compared with other crop types. Notable exceptions, in Australia, are for high oil-producing varieties of lavender, Australian tea-tree (*Melaleuca alternifolia*) and peppermint.

The lavender farm at Lilydale in Tasmania, has run a comprehensive selection program, using extensive field trialling and chemical analysis, for more than 40 years, to choose the cultivars of *Lavandula angustifolia* that are the best yielding and have the highest quality oil. Likewise the Thursday Island tea-tree plantation has run similarly extensive programs to choose the best cultivars of *Melaleuca alternifolia*. These programs have involved considerable time and money, and the companies involved obviously wish to keep control of those cultivars.

If you wish to produce herbal oils, or other herbal chemicals (i.e. for cosmetics or medicines) it is likely that, to compete successfully, you will also have to undertake similar selection programs, and/or to produce oils or chemicals that are not already commonly produced. You may be lucky and be able to obtain some high-yielding cultivars commercially, or from other growers, or from various government organisations (i.e. Department of Agriculture). This will give you a real head start but ideally, further selection using those cultivars as breeding stock is recommended. It is important to note that it is not only necessary to select high yielding cultivars, but also ones that are reasonably easy to grow.

For those who wish to grow a variety of herbs for culinary purposes, then selection programs are not as critical. For nursery production of herbs it is extremely important that the plants you are selling are correctly identified and labelled with their Latin botanical names.

## WHERE TO MARKET YOUR HERB PRODUCTS

### Direct to Retailers
This involves a lot of effort to find retailers who would be interested in your

Choose the cultivars best suited to your purpose, as in this variety of *Lavendula stoechas* (Italian lavender).

product. It has the advantage of cutting out any middle agents, thereby increasing your profit potential.

## Through Wholesalers or Brokers

These have the advantage of having the expertise and contacts to distribute a wide variety of costs. It saves a lot of effort, but of course they want to make a profit so there is less profit than dealing direct.

## Direct Sales

This enables you to sell directly from your property, or perhaps at markets or roadside stalls. This can often be inconvenient as it ties up your time, particularly on weekends when a lot of these types of sales occur. It does however, cut out any middle agent thereby increasing your profit. This can be a good way to sell if you only have small quantities of produce to sell.

## Mail Order

This has proven very successful for 'long life' products and ones that can be easily shipped without damage. Even potted plants have been successfully marketed this way. This method usually involves considerable advertising costs in comparison to the other methods.

Be innovative in the ways that you present your product for sale.

## On contract

This can be direct to perhaps a supermarket chain or to a processing company. Supplying to a processing company means that you will not have to buy expensive processing equipment, but you will also not get the benefit of the value increase in the product after processing.

## EXPORTING YOUR PRODUCE

Another market of increasing importance is the export market. It has been estimated that the USA imports over twenty billion dollars of herbal products per year (Herb Market Report Vol 5, No. 11). There is also increasing concern over the quality of home grown herbal products in Europe. Radioactive fallout from Chernobyl, widespread problems with airborne pollutants and contamination of water supplies, plus the increasing conversion of agricultural land to other uses has led to demand for herbal products from countries that are seen to be 'clean'. Australia is in an ideal situation to capitalise on this situation, in particular providing crops in off season times for the Northern Hemisphere. There is also a small but increasingly strong market for Australian herbs in Asia, particularly fresh culinary herbs.

The prime concerns for exporting crops from Australia is to select the right varieties and to maintain consistent supply and quality. Export agents or brokers are necessary to ensure that your produce is efficiently marketed.

## PRODUCTION REQUIREMENTS

### Land

A successful herb farm could operate on as little as one hectare, or it may require up to a hundred or more hectares depending on the cropping system you are using and the types of plants you are growing. When aiming to buy land consider the following:

SLOPE. Sloping sites often need expensive earth works or levelling before they are suitable for use. For some varieties however, sloping sites are ideal, particularly those that require good drainage.

SOIL. What is the soil like? Is it well structured, well drained, have good fertility and pH, free of pests, weeds and diseases, or other contaminants? Will it need extensive clearance of vegetation or stones?

FLOODING. Is the area prone to flooding?

ACCESS. Is there good access onto the property, through and around the property, and to markets and suppliers?

EXISTING FACILITIES. Does the property have existing facilities that can be utilised in producing your crop? Does the site have power and water either on site, or nearby were it can easily be connected?

CLIMATE. Is the climate suitable for the crops you wish to grow? Are there frost problems, high winds, bushfires, hail, etc?

COST. Are there cheaper alternatives? Can you really afford it? Don't forget that interest rates on loans may rise.

## Equipment and Facilities

Do you have sufficient capital to buy the equipment and facilities needed to produce your crop? Do you have the expertise to use and maintain it?

You will need at least one small tractor and associated implements for soil working, pest and disease control and harvesting and transporting your produce from the field to the processing areas. A vehicle to transport you and your goods will also be required.

You will also need a protected area to work in where you will be able to process your crop, as well as storage areas for supplies, equipment and harvested produce, and toilet facilities for you and your employees. You may have to pay to have electricity and water connected, or you may need to have pumping equipment installed to obtain water from a dam, bore, stream or irrigation channel.

It is important also to have a good source of consumable supplies such as plant stock, fertilisers, pesticides, etc.on site, or nearby where it can easily be contacted?

Careful site planning is required to enable the best use of facilities.

A well-designed potting up bench where soil is easily accessed from a hopper.

## Labour

Sufficient labour is necessary at all times. You may have to arrange for seasonal labour needs (i.e. during processing or harvesting). They must have sufficient expertise (as you must yourself) to produce a good quality crop, and to operate any necessary equipment safely and efficiently.

## COSTING YOUR PRODUCTION

A herb farm, like any business, must set and adhere to certain standards if it is going to operate profitably.

## Cost Efficiency

There must be a sound relationship between cost of production and sales price. Both of these monetary figures must be constantly monitored and maintained at an acceptable level so as to ensure a profitability in the business.

$$\text{Cost of Production} + \text{Profit} = \text{Sales Price}$$

If the cost of production gets too high, then profit will decrease. In such a situation, the sales price must be increased or else the profit figure can become a minus amount (i.e. you might be losing money rather than making money).

In order to control your standard of cost effectiveness, you must understand (and control) all of those things which influence cost of production. You may also need to make adjustments to your sales price figure in order to maintain an acceptable profit figure.

COST OF PRODUCTION. This is influenced by the following factors:
—cost of site (including interest payments, or lease/rent value)
—cost of equipment and facilities both to install and maintain.
—cost of site services (power, gas, water, etc.)
—cost of materials (fertilisers, pesticides, seed, etc.)
—cost of unsold produce. A certain proportion of stock may be lost, may die, or may just become too sick looking to be able to be sold.
—labour costs (be sure to include your own time as well as employees). Labour costs include not only direct wages, but also insurance costs, superannuation payments, holiday pay, sick leave costs, training costs, costs of safety equipment and/or uniforms, etc.
—advertising/promotion (printing, advertising in magazines etc.)
—selling cost (delivering, invoicing, etc.)
—insurance costs such as public liablility, house and property, vehicle, and damage to crops

—taxation (don't forget payroll tax, income tax, etc)

PROFIT. This figure should be over and above money which you earn as wages. If you are only working for wages (with no profit), then you would be better putting your money into some different form of investment and going to work for someone else. Profit should be greater than the interest rate which you could get by investing your money elsewhere. Profit should normally be at least 15–20%. If the business is only small, then the profit margin should be larger. If the business is large, then the profit per unit of produce (e.g. bunch of fresh herbs) can be kept lower. Profit in that situation comes through quantity of sales.

SALES PRICE. The figure which a plant is sold for can vary considerably. Retail price is often about twice wholesale price. This being the case, the wholesaler depends upon selling in large numbers in order to maintain profitability. Wholesale price varies considerably. Generally speaking this figure is largely affected by three things:

—the producer's reliablity of supply. If you are well established and known to be a reliable source of goods, you can often ask a higher price

—quality of plants offered. Higher prices are only paid for top quality stock

—the demand for that particular product. As demand increases prices will generally increase, particularly if supply of the particular product is restricted in some way.

## Quality Standards

The following factors are of concern when considering quality of herbal products:

GENERAL HEALTH. Pest or disease damage, dead leaves, burned leaves, markings on stems etc.

CHEMICAL CONTENT. Herbal products sold for their chemical content may have minimum quantity standards of desirable chemicals and maximum standards for non-desirable chemicals.

UNIFORMITY. Herb plants of a particular variety sold as nursery stock should be in the same-sized pot, the same colour pot, the same type of label, etc. They should all be the same shape and size (roughly).

IMPURITIES. Some products may have a maximum level set for impurities, in particular for products such as dried herbs.

AGE OF PRODUCT. Use-by dates may be applied to some products, particularly culinary and medicinal to ensure their freshness.

## Size Standards

Many products will have minimum and/or maximum size standards apply. For example bunches of fresh herbs should be of a certain size or weight.

## PRACTICAL EXERCISE

1. Consider the formula:
Cost of Production + Profit = Sales Price

2. Plan the establishment of a new hypothetical herb farm which is to produce bunches of fresh culinary herbs for sale to local fruit and vegetable stores and restaurants.

3. Set a sales price per bunch of herbs to be produced (be realistic).
Sales Price = $.......... per bunch

4. Set a profit figure for the formula (probably 20 or 30% of sales price, depending on the scale of production).
Profit = $.......... per bunch

5. Calculate what your cost of production should be.
Cost of Production (per bunch) = $..........

6. On the basis of the cost of production you have set, prepare a simple budget for the first year's operation of this herb farm.
Fill in costs below:

BUDGET
Number of bunches to be produced in the first year...........................

Number of bunches to be thrown away (die, become diseased, get too woody etc.).........................

Number of bunches sold in first year.........................

Money generated through sales (income)...........................

Cost of Production
| | |
|---|---|
| Property and Services | $....... |
| Materials | $....... |
| Pots | $....... |
| Soil | $....... |
| Fertiliser | $....... |
| Other chemicals | $....... |
| Stationery | $....... |

| | |
|---|---|
| Labour | $....... |
| Advertising/Promotion | $....... |
| Selling | $....... |
| Other | $....... |
| | |
| Total Operating Costs = | $....... |

NOW ..... Consider how efficient your planned operation is.

What things could you look at to increase your profitability?

What costs might be reduced?

By thinking through these things you will develop your insight into more efficient business management.

## Hypothetical Case Study

1. Consider the formula...
Cost of Production + Profit = Sales Price

2. Plan the establishment of a new hypothetical herb farm which is to produce bunches of fresh culinary herbs for sale to local fruit & vegetable stores and restaurants.
3. Set a sales price per bunch of herbs to be produced (be realistic).
Sales Price = 90 cents per bunch

4. Set a profit figure for the formula (probably 40 or 50% of sales price, depending on the scale of production).
Profit = 45 cents per bunch

5. Calculate what your cost of production should be.
Cost of Production (per bunch) = 45 cents

6. On the basis of the cost of production you have set, prepare a simple budget for the first year's operation of this herb farm.
Fill in costs below:

BUDGET
Number of bunches to be produced in the first year = 65,000

Number of bunches to be thrown away = 5,000 (die, become diseased, etc.)

Number of bunches sold in first year = 60,000

Money generated through sales (income) = $54,000

Cost of Production
| | |
|---|---|
| Property and Services | $8,000 |
| Materials | $3,000 |
| Fertilizer | $3,000 |
| Other chemicals | $800 |
| Stationery | $400 |
| Labour | $26,000 |
| Transport/Marketing | $2,300 |
| Vehicle Expenses | $5,300 |
| Other (e.g. insurance) | $1,200 |

Total Operating Costs =            $50,000        Profit = $4,000

Are these figures realistic?
How could each cost be lowered?
Is the profit enough, or would you be better off investing elsewhere?

# History of a Nursery

One of the most important points to remember is that skill and knowledge are essential in the operation of a good nursery or herb farm. If you don't have the skill yourself, you are better advised to start small, perhaps just as a hobby; learn from your experiences and gradually grow into the type of operation you desire or employ a skilled person right from the beginning.

## History of a Nursery

The following chronology could easily be the way a nursery grows from a hobby into a thriving small business.

FEBRUARY 1st year. Move into a new home, decide there is a need to get interested in gardening, join a night course, hear a lecture on propagation and decide to experiment at home. 'Maybe I can grow my own plants and save having to buy them.'

NOVEMBER 3rd year. Propagating plants has become such a keen hobby that this year's tax return cheque is spent on buying a small hobby glasshouse.

JANUARY 4th year. More than 50 per cent of the plants being propagated die overnight due to a damping-off disease. The dead plants are taken to Department of Agriculture and the problem discovered. All of a sudden there is a realisation that there is more to propagation than meets the eye.

MARCH 4th year. Commence studying night classes to learn more. Buy texts, read profusely on everything from pest control to plant identification and soils. Join a couple of garden clubs. Continue to experiment and propagate at home.

SEPTEMBER 5th year. Develop a keen interest in eucalypts. Collect and sow seed of as many different eucalypts as possible. Also grow a variety of other plants from both Australia and overseas. Have a strong motivation to grow things not grown previously. Most of the plants grown to date have been either given away to close friends, charities or family.

APRIL 6th year. A friend of a friend telephones, says he is looking for plants for a new home and is willing to pay for them. When he comes around, he buys a lot of shrubs and ground cover but only a few trees, saying he isn't interested in the wide variety of eucalypts which have been grown. It is realised that 'Maybe I can make a living out of this hobby' but also that 'Not everything is saleable'.

The money from the sale is used to buy a propagating bed. The decision is made to become more serious about the hobby.

AUGUST 6th year. While talking to a nurseryman, who is a fellow member of a garden club, decide to show him some plants with the prospect of selling them.

SEPTEMBER 6th year. The nurseryman buys a few hundred plants but advises that he would pay more if they were in standard containers, in a lighter weight soil mix and all labelled with printed plant labels.

JANUARY 7th year. Over the summer vacation break, draw up plans and a schedule for what will be grown over that year. Income and expenditure is planned and time is allocated to various tasks on the basis that one day and four nights a week will be spent in developing the nursery.

JUNE 8th year. The backyard is full of plants (more than 12,000). They are selling but not fast enough. A shop site in the local shopping centre is seen to be for sale or lease.

JULY 1978. The shop site is leased and fencing paid for with savings from plant sales. With the help of friends and family, everything is moved from the backyard to the shop. The wife runs the shop during the week and the husband takes over at weekends. He still hold his job.

NOVEMBER 8th year. After a slow start, people are getting to know the nursery and earnings are around the average weekly wage in profit each week (for 7 days' work) after paying the rent and other expenses. After visits from Hortico, Yates, Thompson & Morgan, Attunga etc. a small range of fertilisers, chemicals, seed and soil mixes is stocked.

JANUARY 9th year. Everyone in the area has gone on holidays and the weekly profit (for 7 days' work) is very low.

FEBRUARY 1979. A decision is made to advertise in a couple of garden magazines. People are back from holidays and the advertisements pay off. By the end of February, weekly profits are almost up to those of spring.

MARCH 9th year. The advertising continues to pay off. Weekly profits are now increasing. Taking a gamble, the husband resigns his job and puts his full-time effort into the nursery, taking charge of propagation while the wife sells.

OCTOBER 9th year. After a slack period in winter, sales have improved in spring and the weekly earnings, after expenses, have increased further.

The type of evolution outlined above is by no means the only way for a nursery of herb farm to develop, but it is probably the most common story. Sometimes people don't go much beyond that initial development into a small part-time backyard operation. There is, amongst some established nursery owners, animosity towards the 'backyarder', the argument normally being that they are 'unprofessional'. This can sometimes make it hard to break into the business. If the beginner can present himself and his product in a more professional or polished way, this problem is usually easily overcome.

Perhaps the most important point of all to remember in the early stages is not to rush. It is safer to allow plant and business expertise to build up slowly and surely.

# Nursery Profile

TYPE. Propagation and growing on to medium sizes (14 cm).

STAFFING. One well-trained manager (full-time); owners (husband and wife) do potting and other manual work weekends only; additional casual help employed occasionally.

YEAR OF OPERATION. Just commencing third.

LOCATION. Near Woodend, Victoria.

EQUIPMENT AND FACILITIES. Two heated glasshouses with automatic irrigation, heating/misting beds for propagation, shadehouse, steam soil sterilisation, 45,000-litre water tank, average size dam and pumping right from reliable creek, 0.4 ha growing-on area (only small proportion currently used), 0.4 ha garden for stock plants, approximately 2.5 ha of bush which could be used for expansion.

MARKETING. Truck sales to retail nurseries and contract sales, mainly to country nurseries in Victoria and Southern NSW.

VARIETIES GROWN. Advertise anything, seem to concentrate on exotic shrubs and trees.

POTTING MIX. Varies. Components include mountain soil, granitic sand, lignite and scoria (all obtainable locally).

ANNUAL PRODUCTION. To date a major part of the work has been put into developing facilities, thus turnover still is below 20,000 13–15 cm pots. This will increase to at least 50,000 or 60,000 in the current year.

LAYOUT. See plan on page 25. Note that access to all parts of the nursery is excellent and flow between areas is good.

# Herb Farm Profile

TYPE. Container plants and herbal pest-control sprays.

STAFFING. Husband and wife owners plus one full-time nursery hand (i.e. three full-time staff).

TIME OF OPERATION. Well established, more than five years.

LOCATION. Western District, Victoria.

EQUIPMENT AND FACILITIES. Small simple glasshouse, approx. 350 m² of shadehouse, approx. 50 m² of shed (used in making up sprays), 0.2 ha display/experimental herb garden, large dam.

Tahara Farm, a successful farm, one of the first to develop herb products for home gardeners in Australia.

MARKETING. Truck sales of plants to nurseries in Western Victoria and Geelong. Retailing at wholesale prices to general public from the nursery. Herb sprays sold mainly through a horticultural product distribution company in Melbourne.

VARIETIES GROWN. Approximately 200 types of herbs plus a range of permaculture/crop plants.

POTTING MIX. All local components including compost, scoria, soil, sand etc.

ANNUAL PRODUCTION. The major part of the business comes from sale of the herb sprays. Container plant production tends to vary but a stock of between 5,000 and 10,000 is usually maintained on hand.

# Bibliography

Kenneth F. Baker, *The U.C System for Producing Healthy Container-Grown Plants,* University of California, 1957.

RJ. Garner, *The Grafters Handbook,* Faber & Faber, London, 1979.

Handreck, K & Black, N. *Growing Media For Ornamental Plants and Turf,* NSW University Press, Sydney, 1984.

H. Hartmann & D. Kester,*Plant Propagation: Principles and Practice,* 4th edn, Prentice Hall, Engelwood Cliffs, New Jersey, 1983.

H. Hartmann, W. Flocker & A. Kofranek, *Plant Science: Growth, Development and Utilization of Cultivated Plants,* Prentice Hall, Engelwood Cliffs, New Jersey, 1981.

Hillier & Sons, *Hillier's Manual of Trees and Shrubs,* 5th edn, David and Charles, Devon, UK, 1981.

International Plant Propagators Society (IPPS) Combined Proceedings.

Macdonald B. *Practical Woody Plant Propagation for Nursery Growers,* Timber Press, 1986.

John Mason, *Plant Nutrition,* PCH Australia, Melbourne, 1978.

John Mason, *Commercial Hydroponics,* Kangaroo Press, 1990.

John Mason, *Growing Herbs,* Kangaroo Press, 1993.

John Mason, *Tropical & Warm Climate Gardening,* Bay Books, 1995.

John Mason, *Yates Guide to Pests & Diseases,* Angus & Robertson, 1995.

John Mason, *Nursery Management,* Kangaroo Press, 1994.

John Mason, *Farm Management,* Kangaroo Press, 1996.

John Mason, *Growing Pelargoniums and Geraniums,* Hyland House, 1996.

John Mason, *Sustainable Farming,* Kangaroo Press, 1997.

John Stanely & Alan Toogood, *The Modern Nurseryman,* Faber & Faber, London, 1981.

*Many of the above publications are available from the author, John Mason, at the Australian Horticultural Correspondence School, 264 Swansea Rd, Lilydale, Vic,3140. Ph: (03) 9736 1882, or PO Box 2092, Nerang East, Qld, 4211. Ph: (07) 5530 4855.*

# Directory

This is by no means a comprehensive directory, but may give you some guide if you have no other contacts.

### Glasshouses and Shadehouses
Sage Horticultural (Greenhouse, hydroponic and propagation supplies),
  121 Herald St, Cheltenham, 3192. Ph: (03) 9553 3777, fax: (03) 9555 3013.
Solar Hot Houses, Wallenjoe Rd, Epsom, Vic 3551.  Ph: (03) 5488 8494.
One Stop Sprinklers, 645 Burwood Hwy, Vermont Sth, Vic 3133. Ph: (03) 9800 2177,
  (03) 5774 0665.
Greenhouse Building Materials, 69 Canterbury Rd, Canterbury, NSW 2193.
Econo Greenhouse P/L, 201 Darling St, Balmain, NSW 2041.
Commercial Glasshouses, 39 Barry St, Kellyville, NSW 2153.
VP Industries (Tunnel Buildings), PO Box 301, Beenleigh, Qld 4207. Ph: (07) 3287 1088,
  fax: (07) 807 3675.
BMB Industries, Beachmere Rd, Caboolture, Qld 4510. Ph: (07) 5492 2977.
John Falland Aust, Moppa Rd Sth, Nurioopta, SA 5355.  Ph: (08) 8562 1533.

### Hormones
Kendon Chemical Co, 71 McClure St, Thornbury, Vic 3071.
Fertool Distributors, 97 Abbott Rd, Hallam, Vic 3803.
Fernland Agencies, P.O. Box 5054, Nambour, Qld 4560.  Ph: (07) 5441 1711.
Globe Aust. P/L, 163 Port Hacking Rd, Miranda, NSW 2228.  Ph: (02) 9522 0000.
Growth Technology (Clonex, Nutrients, Growth kits), 244 South St. South Freemantle, WA 6162.
  Ph: (08) 9430 4713

### Mechanical Aids/Propagating Equipment
Sage Horticultural (Greenhouse, hydroponic and propagation supplies), 121 Herald St, Cheltenham,
  Vic 3192. Ph: (03) 9553 377, fax: (03) 9555 3013.
Irelands Hydroponics & Horticultural Lighting, 31 Main St, Kinglake, Vic 3763.
  Ph: (03) 5786 1443, fax: (03) 5786 1286.
Berwick Climate Control, 6/16 Melverton Dve, Hallam, Vic 3803.
C & M Innovations, Unit 19/7 Hanlon Cl, Minto, NSW 2566.
Gold Coast Hydroponics, Shop 301, Australia Fair, Scarborough St, (PO Box 3407) Southport,
  Qld 4215.  Ph: (07) 5591 6380.
Aqua-ponics WA, Lot 12 Warton Rd, Canningvale, WA 6155. Ph: (08) 9455 2133.
Adelaide Hydroponics, 21 Tapleys Hill Rd, Hendon, SA 5014. Ph: (08) 8240 0423.

## Potting and Propagating Media

Propine (Media and fertilisers), 160 Colchester Rd, Kilsyth, Vic 3137. Ph: (03) 9728 2588,
   fax: (03) 9728 1848
Growool (Rockwool), 159 Wellington Rd, Clayton, Vic 3168.
Australian Hydroponics (Rockwool), Silver St, Collingwood, Vic Ph: (03) 9419 1699
Red Top Distributors (Vermiculite), 39 Horne St, Elsternwick,Vic 3185. Ph: (03) 9528 4044
Australian Perlite, 20 McPherson St, Banksmeadow, NSW 2019.
Searle P/L, PO Box 183, Kilcoy, Qld 4515. Ph: (074) 97 2022.
Amgrow P/L, PO Box 1085, Penrith, NSW 2750. Ph: (02) 29 0470

## Pots/Containers

Garden City Plastics (Pots), Cramms Rd, Monbulk, Vic 3793.
   2/10 Veronica St, Capalaba, Qld 4517. Ph. (07) 3245 2422
Gale Aust, 270 Bay Rd, Cheltenham, Vic 3192. Ph: (03) 9583 3333
Reko P/L, P.O. Box 795, Gosford, NSW 2250. Ph: (02) 4328 1599
Plastamatic, 3 Graham Rd, Highett, Vic 3190. Ph: (03) 9555 5111
Agricultural Plastics (Grow Bags), 6 Airds Rd, Minto, NSW 2566. Ph: 008 224 207
Pacific World Packaging (Pots), 21 Provident Ave, Glynde, SA 5070. Ph: (08) 8337 7355,
   1247 Boundary Rd, Wacol, Qld 4076. Ph: (07) 3271 1700,
   344 Annangrove Rd, Rouse Hill, NSW 2155. Ph: (02) 9679 1333
Amec Plastics, 16 Hutchinson St, Burleigh, Qld 4220. Ph: (07) 5593 5905
Statewide Nursery Supplies, 32 Tenbar St, Tingalpa, Qld 4173. Ph: (07) 3849 8912

## Selected Seed Suppliers

Arthur Yates & Co, 244-254 Horsley Rd, Milperra, NSW, 2214. Ph: (02) 9588 2222,
   fax: (02) 9588 3030. Wide range of varieties, including flowers, perennials and cut flowers.
Attunga Horticultural Co, 57 Radford Rd, Reservoir, Vic 3073. Ph: (03) 9460 7244. Packaged
   vegetable and flower seeds.
Cropcare, 40 Janet Rd, Safety Bay, WA 6169. Ph: (08) 9527 8442, fax: (08) 9350 5862. Flowers,
   vegetables, herbs, palms, trees, shrubs & ferns.
Dessert R. B. Seed Co, PO Box 497 Kununurra, WA 6743. Ph: (08) 9168 2122.
   Herbs, flowers, vegetables, grasses, legumes.
Diggers Seeds, 105 Latrobe Parade, Dromana, Vic,3936. Ph: (03) 5987 1519.
   Wide range of vegetable, flower and perennial seeds.
Eden Seeds, MS 316 Gympie, Qld 4570. Ph: (07) 5486 5230.
   Non-hybrid flower, perennial and shrub seeds.
Erica Vale Seeds, PO Box 50, Jannali, NSW, 2226. Ph: (02) 9533 3593.
   Wide range of seeds, in particular flower and vegetable.
Fruit Spirit Botanical Garden, C\- Dorroughby PO, NSW, 2480. Ph: (02) 6689 5192.
   Fruits, nuts, gingers, bamboos, etc.
Goodmans Seeds, PO Box 91, Bairnsdale, Vic 3875. Ph: (03) 5152 4060, fax: (03) 5152 1671.
   Wide variety of flower and vegetable seeds.
Greenline Nursery, PO Box 2486, Mt Gambier, SA 5290.
   Aust native tree, flowers, vegetables and herb seeds.
Green Harvest, 52 Crystal Waters, MS 16, Maleny, Qld 4552.
Jerd Seeds, 140 Madden Ave, Mildura, Vic 3500. Ph: Free call (1800) 803 383,
   also 1 Orchid Crt, Park Orchards, Vic 3114. Ph: (03) 9876 1525.

Kings Herb Seeds, PO Box 975, Penrith, NSW 2751. Ph: (047) 761 493
  Wide variety of herb, vegetable and flower varieties.
Lorraine Blaney, Wallace Rd, Beachmere, Qld 4510.
  Unusual herbs, spices, Asian & oriental vegetables, and cottage garden plants from open pollinated flowers.
Mr Fothergill's Seeds, 5/16 Garling Rd, Kings Park, NSW 2148. Ph: (02) 9831 2919.
New Gippsland Seed Farm, Queens Rd, Silvan, Vic 3795. Ph: (03) 9737 9560.
  Vegetable seed suppliers.
Northrup King Seeds, PO Box 335, Dandenong, Vic 3175. Ph: (03) 9706 3033,
  fax: (03) 9706 3182. Wide range, including flowers, vegetables and perennials.
Richter Herb Seeds, Lot 3488 Quin Rd, Gin Gin, WA 6503. Ph: (08) 9575 7522,
  fax: (08) 9575 7622.
Specialty Seeds, Hawthorn Park, Chanters Lane, Tylden, Vic 3444.
Supa-Pak Seeds, 38 Shelgate St, Chermside West, Qld 4032. Ph: (07) 3359 2410,
  fax: (07) 3359 2410. Packet vegetable, flower and herb seeds.

## International Seed Merchants

Colegrave Seeds Ltd, West Adderbury, Banbury, Oxon OX173EY, UK.
  Ph: Banbury (0295) 810632, fax: (0295) 811833. Flower seed specialists.
Silverhill Seeds, 18 Silverhill Crescent, Kenilworth, 7700, South Africa. Ph: (21) 762 4245,
  fax: (21) 797 6609. Specialist in South African natives. Proteaceae, Ericaceae, Geraniaceae, bulbs, succulents, annuals, perennials, trees & shrubs. Catalogue available.
Kings Herb Seeds (New Zealand), PO Box 19-084, Avondale, Auckland, New Zealand.
  Ph: (09) 887 588, fax: (09) 828 7588. Wide variety of herb, vegetable and flower seeds.
A.L. Tozers Seeds, Pyports, Cobham, Surrey, KT11 3EH, UK.
  Ph: (0932) 62059, fax: (0932) 68973. Vegetable & flower seeds.
Hamer Flower Seeds, Sheraton House, Office 29, Castle Park, Cambridge, CB3 0AX, UK,
  Ph: (0223) 327520, fax: (0223) 462542.
Breeders Seeds, 17 Summerwood Lane, Halsall, Ormskirk, Lancs, L39 8RQ, UK.
  Ph: (0704) 840775, fax: (0704) 841099. Flower & vegetable seed.
E.W. King & Co, Monks Farm, Kelvedon, Essex, C05 9PG, UK. Ph: (0376) 570000. Vegetable
  seeds.
Elsoms Seeds, Ph: Spalding (0775) 711911, fax: (0775) 723209. Distributor for several European
  seed merchants.
Pinetree Vandenberg, Lower Rd, Effingham. Leatherhead, Surrey KT24 5JP, UK.
  Ph: (0372) 456688, fax: (0372) 452857. Vegetables (lettuce).
Clause UK Ltd, Ph: (061) 4866872, fax: (061) 4866874. Iceberg lettuces.
Enza Zaden UK Ltd, Plantation House, Milber Trading Estate, Newton Abbot, Devon TQ12 4SG,
  UK. Ph: (0626) 333616, fax: (0626) 331457. Vegetables (ie: lettuce).
Booker Seeds, Boston Rd, Sleaford, Lincolnshire NG34 7HA, UK.
  Ph: (0529) 304511, fax: (0529) 303908. Vegetable seeds.

## Associations

International Plant Propagators Society
  Membership is open to anyone, whether amateur or professional, who propagates plants and who wishes to seek and share knowledge and experiences with other propagators from around the world.
  c/- Francis Biggs, P.O. Box 124, North Richmond, NSW, 2654. Ph: (02) 4571 1321

# Australian Horticultural Correspondence School

The Australian Correspondence Schools conduct more than 250 different home study courses including eleven courses designed for people who work, or would like to work, in nurseries. These range from courses for people who propagate plants at home as a small part time business, to courses designed for managers or owners of large commercial operations. The three certificates offered are all government accredited, and as such, well accepted by both industry and other educational institutions.

## Courses offered include:
**Short Courses:** Propagation, Advanced Propagation, Tissue Culture, Nursery Growers Course, Nursery HandsCourse, Soil Management (Nurseries), Garden Centre Management, Wholesale Nursery Management
**Accredited Certificates:** Certificate in Horticulture (Propagation), Advanced Certificate in Applied Management (Retail Nursery), Advanced Certificate in Applied Management (Wholesale Nursery)

The Nursery Growers Course is an 80 hour introductory course for people starting a small, part time business, growing and selling plants. This is a course for the inexperienced grower only.

Garden Centre Management and Wholesale Nursery Management are 120 hour courses, each providing a basic training for nurserymen who might not have the time to pursue a full certificate.

The Certificate in Horticulture (Propagation) is similar to other horticulture certificates in its introductory (core) units, but devotes 50% of the course to quite different topics, specifically related to propagation. Designed principally for plant propagators, this course deals with hundreds of different types of plants and the methods used to propagate them.

The Advanced Certificate in Applied Management (Retail Nursery) is devoted equally to developing management and horticultural skills for a supervisor or manager in a retail nursery or garden centre. The key areas of study are: Communications, Management, Office Practices, Business Operations, Marketing, Plant Identification and Culture, Nursery Plant Stock, Nursery Production Systems and Equipment, Display & Display Techniques and Garden Product Knowledge (Hardware).

Advanced Certificate in Applied Management (Wholesale Nursery) covers Communications, Management, Office Practices, Business Operations, Marketing, Plant Identification and Culture,Propagation, and Nursery Production Systems and Equipment.

Advanced Diploma in Horticulture (Nursery). Recognised in Australia by accreditation authorities, at the time of publication this is the highest level professional qualification available in Australia's Vocational Education System. It takes 3 years full-time or 5–7 years part-time to complete and is available only through this school.

Other certificate and non-certificate courses are offered in related disciplines including, Herbs, Horticultural Technology, Landscaping, Small Business, Supervision and Marketing, Irrigation, and Soil Management.

**VIDEOS**
The school also produces horticultural videos on a range of topics including Herb Identification and Propagation. A full list is available on request.

For further details contact:
Australian Correspondence Schools
P.O. Box 2092, Nerang East, Queensland, Australia, 4211.
Phone: (07) 5530 4855.
E-mail address: acs@qldnet.com.au

Swansea Rd, Lilydale, Victoria, Australia, 3140.
Phone: (03) 9736 1882.
E-mail address: acs@onthe.net.au

Web Sites
Horticulture and Gardening Web Site     http://www.qldnet.com.au/acs/hort
Correspondence School Web Site          http://www.qldnet.com.au/acs

# Glossary

**Bare Rooted** These are plants that have been 'lifted' from their growing area without the soil or growing media left around their roots. This is common for many deciduous ornamental trees (eg: elms, ashes, maples) and fruit trees (eg: apricot, apple, peach, pear), and shrubs such as roses. The plants should be planted as soon as possible to prevent the roots drying out. They can be temporarily stored if the roots are covered with a moist material such as peat moss, straw, or rotted sawdust.

**Bedding Plants** These are plants used for temporary displays, generally planted out in warmer seasons (eg: many annuals).

**Bottom Heat** This is where heat is applied at, or near, the base of plants to stimulate growth. This can be done in a variety of ways, including under bench heating with heat cables or hot water pipes, heating of floors in greenhouses using heat cables, or composting materials such as sawdust or manures. (See also **Hotbed**.)

**Coldframe** This is in effect a mini-greenhouse. Generally unheated, they are commonly used to provide protection for plants being propagated, or for plants that may need a short period of protection against extremes of climate. They have the advantage of being readily moveable, and easy to construct.

**Dibble Stick** This is a short pencil-like stick that is used to make holes in growing media for the potting-up ('pricking out') of seedlings, or for inserting or potting-up cuttings.

**Flats** These are shallow trays with drainage holes in the bottom, which are commonly for germinating seeds, or rooting cuttings.

**Forcing** The use of heat and altered light conditions to induce very early flowering, or very tall growth. Commonly used in cut flower production.

**Growing Media** Any material in which plants are being grown can be classified as a growing media. This includes soil, soilless potting mixes, rockwool, vermiculite, even water (ie: hydroponics).

**Hotbed** This is a bed used for plant propagation that provides heat to the base of seed trays or to pots of cuttings to stimulate germination in seedlings and subsequent root growth, and root initiation and growth in cuttings. Heat is normally supplied from either hot water pipes, or from resistance cables which, when an electric current is passed through them, heat up. These heating elements generally have some material such as propagating sand, vermiculite, gravel or perlite placed around them to help spread (diffuse) the heat.

**Juvenility** A stage of a plant's life following the germination of a seed to produce a seedling. Vegetative growth dominates, and juvenile plants can't respond to flower-inducing stimuli. In some plants juvenile foliage differs markedly from adult foliage (eg: some eucalypts). In difficult-to-root plants taking cutting material from stock plants in a juvenile phase will often give better results than using older (adult growth phase) material.

**Living Colour** Plants cultivated to provide colourful displays (ie: foliage, flowers, fruit). These can be either in ground or in containers, and be grown for either short- or long-term display.

**Micropropagation** This is the production (propagation) of plants from very small plant parts, tissues or cells. They are grown under aseptic conditions in a highly controlled environment. The term 'tissue culture' is a collective term used to describe a number of in-vitro procedures used in culturing plant tissue, including producing haploid plant cells and artificial hybridisation.

**Plugs** These are individual plants, or small clumps of plants, that are grown in trays containing large numbers of individual cells. For example, the tray may have 18 cells (across) by 32 cells (along), making a total 576 cells per tray, with each individual cell having measuring 20 x 20 mm and with a depth of 30 mm. Each cell having an individual drainage hole. The trays are filled with a growing media and seed is planted into each cell, either by hand (very slow) or by machine.

There are machines that are capable of planting individual seeds into each cell, and very quickly. The trays are made of plastic, that has some degree of flexibility so that it can be bent a little to allow easy removal of individual plugs (root ball and growing media combined). This type of growing system, is ideal for flower and vegetable seedlings, and can be highly mechanised (eg: filling trays with soil, seeding, potting up individual plugs).

**Potted Colour** Plants grown in containers to provide a colourful display. They are commonly used as an alternative to cut flowers (eg: chrysanthemums in 150 mm pots), and are generally discarded once their peak display (eg: flowering) has finished.

**Provenance** This is also known as 'seed origin' and refers to where the seed has been produced. This can give an indication of the particular genetic characteristics of the seed (eg: size, shape, flower colour, adaptation to climatic conditions, resistance to pest and diseases, tolerance to different soil conditions).

**Scarification** This is any process that breaks, scratches, cuts, mechanically alters, or softens seed coats to make them more permeable to water and gases. Techniques include dipping in hot water, dipping in concentrated sulphuric acid, removing hard seed coats with sand paper, and nicking seed coats with a sharp knife.

**Standards** These are where plants are grown as a single tall stem (e.g: some fruit trees & roses). Some prostrate cultivars are also budded or grafted onto taller stemmed rootstocks to create pendulous forms (eg: weeping elm, *Grevillea* 'Gaudi-chaudi' and 'Royal Mantle').

**Stock Plants** These are the parent plants from which cutting propagation material is obtained. There are three main sources of stock plant material. These are i) plants growing in parks, around houses, in the wild, etc. ii) prunings or trimmings from young nursery plants, and iii) plants grown specifically as a source of cutting material. Stock plants should be correctly identified (and true to type), and in a healthy condition.

**Stratification** This is where dormant seeds, that have imbibed water, are subjected to a period of chilling to 'after-ripen' the embryo. This process is also known as moist-chilling. Dry seeds should be soaked in water prior to stratification. Seeds are then usually mixed with some sort of moisture retaining material, such as coarse washed sand, or peat or sphagnum moss, or vermiculite. The material should be moistened prior to mixing. The mix is then stored at a temperature of 0–10ºC. The lower shelf of a domestic refrigerator is usually suitable. The time of stratification will depend on seed type, but usually 1–4 months. In areas with cool winters, stratification can be carried out in beds outdoors, but seeds should be protected from pests such as birds, or mice.

**Tissue Culture** see **Micropropagation**

**Tubes**   Small, narrow containers, commonly used for the first potting-up stage of newly propagated seed or cuttings. The tube-like nature encourages new roots to grow straight down, reducing the risk of roots coiling. A common tube used in Australia has an upper diameter of 50 mm, a depth of around 70 mm, tapering down to a lower diameter of about 40 mm. This type is most widely used in producing stock for planting up into larger containers. Deeper tubes are also commonly used for tubing up quick-growing seedlings that are to be used in large scale plantings (eg: reafforestation, farms, trees). Some nurseries specialise in just tubestock production for sale to other nurseries, for growing on.

**Tubestock**   Plants grown in tube-like containers (see **Tubes** above).

**Wounding**   Root production on cuttings can often be promoted by wounding the base of cuttings. A common method of wounding plants is to cut away a thin strip of bark, about 1.5 to 3 cm long (this will depend on the size of the cutting) from each side of the cutting near the base. The strip should not be cut too deeply, just enough to expose the cambium layer (the soft layer of new growth between the wood and the bark), without cutting very deeply into the wood beneath.

# Index